what the trees hide

a collection of poetry and lyrical scribblings

by

Dydda

Firstly, this book is dedicated to all the lost souls in search of rest. You withered High Schooler, trying to learn how to cope with chemical overloads. You starving soldiers in a love war. You self-esteemless woman in need of a mirror that shows the beauty of your heart, instead of the "flaws" of your skin. You suicidal misfit, searching for release from the ache of life's needle. You cold living-dead, needing to feel anything besides nothing. You addicts of the poison well, praying for sobriety. The only salvation from this worthless life, is the salvation from a perfect Christ. And without your struggles, I would not be here, my friends. All of this is for you.

Secondly, this book is dedicated to the memory of Alexandria Dawn Pease. I pray the words in this book reflect the beauty of your soul. Rest in peace, Dear, and "Above all else, never forget to love..."

Table of Contents

"Do not be overcome by evil, but overcome evil with good..."

-romans twelve twenty one

act one

pathos

Baize

Roses   are   dead
Violets are   crude
I hate   people
But   I   love   you

N-hail X-hail

In the time we have left
        Let's not fight about who's wrong and who's right
In the time we have
        Let us search the star-strewn sky
For our favorite sun, a trillion lifetimes away
        And let us celebrate
The birth of that solar-flare
        That brought us here
Let us leave aside our fears
        And celebrate that spark of life
Even as we fade into the growing night
        There is a special place inside
That can set us free
        If we accept it and breathe
Just breathe
        And release all other needs
Together, we'll learn to breathe
        Again...

Gagfly

Sticky crime scenes
    Wads of tobacco and hair
        The air is thick with humidity
           Curling tissue paper

           Flashes of bulb lightning
        The 40 watt was no joke
    Or maybe 35...
The flies begin to choke

Lost teeth, hiding from the crippled
    On the tile floor
        Swollen virgins with stars in a bucket
           Stagnant and sore

           Coughing up dust and cremation ash
        Make a victimless world and I'll show you the eyes
    Of past eternities, draped in a silken stash
Milk spoiled, lust and lies

Turn from your false identity
    Idolized and traumatized
        This is your Adonis sea
           Hospitalized for attempts at suicide

        I was there when you took your first breath

And I'll be there when take your last
You just need to trust in me and I'll give you rest
Your past is forgotten, cause your past is just that

Amnesia

Spiritual   drought

Name your doubt right

now

Elijah hears it is going to

rain

Who operates like it's going to

rain?

Go tell the king, it's down the

drain

Faith is the substance of things hoped

for

Change   the way you speak

I   don't have a car yet but I'm going to clean out my garage

Make a   sacrifice

Leave something behind so I can have something   better

1   King 18:18ff

How   long will you respond with not a word to something God is

Calling   you to?

If   you want to grow you will need to get the sin out

Indecision for the vision will cause a ministry with   division

Divided   loyalties

Our God uses fire to put out   water

If you're going to go to the altar you're going to have   to

sacrifice   something

Make   it about the inside

Verse   41. There's no rain but he hears that it's coming

Can't   you hear it?

14

Spiritual   healing

Forgiveness

Get people to help see the   birth

Vs   42-43

There is   nothing

Seven   times

You need others to help you keep   looking

You have to be willing to go back and   look

Go   back

Keep   looking

I don't know how many times it's going to   take

Go   with even the smallest of blessings

Vs   44. It's small

We   did all we did and this is all we got?

You're   disappointed in what you have received

Prepare   your chariot

Thank   your God for the little you have received

Heavy   rain

Monoxide

When the curtains open
When self-worth takes center stage
My selfishness is stinking and the neighbors know there's
somethin- g wrong
They could never guess, n- o they could never understand
I rewrite my story
Just so I don't hav- e to read this ending
Cause there's no happily ever after for sinners like me
No, my lig- hts go out
My candles ar- e buried alive
Can you hear t- hem burning?
Can you see them screaming?
My candles are buried, a- nd I have no one left to blame

When the ba- ttle's lost
When the smok- e is blown away
I can see my hearts- trings stretch out like a map
Filling the valle- ys with empty veins
Crawling beneath m- y skin is blue bodies
Like cold oceans tha- t swallow drunken sailors
They ignored the warnin- gs because they knew better
Yes, they all knew better so they didn't head towards the
bay when the sto- rm heads rolled in

Threadbare souls with impure edges
Solid state with n- o warmth in their bones

Why can't I have enemies?
They all turned to frie- nds that were oh, so concerned
But when I pushed them a- way, why don't they hate me?
Why does everyone forgive me when it's the one thing I
can ne- ver do?
I feel their words of acc- eptance writhe beneath my skin
And my stomach ca- n't hold down their love

Does it make you feel ali- ve when the car is started in
the dark?
With closed doors in the garage there's no escape from
Monoxid- e kisses
I close my eyes for the final goodbye
And I know if I ever open them, I'll never forgive myself

Ishtar

Shindler's fist

Found fighting against

The resistance

A revolutionary Renascence

Broken bottles and decadence

Floating a sea of perfume

A blood flower blooms

CEO fumes

Like a cremation

Exasperation

Imagination

Pre-procreation

Sold socialization

A burden of the diarchy

Confessions of a confederate

Sweet tea and sweeties

Meet your meat

Call the call

My reality is my creativity

Balanced on a glass ship of anarchy

Punk rock

At Fort Knox

Barbie look-a-like contest

Feel yourself find it, find this

Your calendar is scot-free

Son of a shepherd, fishing for blasphemers in American society

Moist

Filled
    to the brim with foaming emptiness

Spinning
    on the score of surrenderin'

Scribbled
    smiles on your face to pretend
    That it doesn't hurt to breathe the ash in
    Crazy as the straw you use to suck my heart out with
    Seems like only yesterday you were on oxygen
    You savored every last dew drop of my sickness

Filled
    to the brim with ecstasy and forgiven for my symptoms

Trenches

Funeral

Ecclesiastes

Time to be born

David said we are FEARFULLY and WONDERFULLY made

There   is   a   time   to   die

We are all appointed to   death

A life on this earth will come to an   end

Be ready to   go

David, our lives are like a flower in a field

Life begins with birth and ends with   death

                                        Sorrow

                                Remembrance

        Celebration

        Unique   things about this person

                                        Conversations, encounters

        Simple   moments

        Common   ground

        Importance   of home

        Fun

                                                Jobs

                                        Military

                                        Church

        Salvation

Paul to be absent from the body is to be present with The Lord

                                We'll be with him again

Jesus   has gone to prepare a place

   His life has an everlasting effect because of his decision
to follow The Lord

                   How people who live for The Lord deal with death

Comfort

Strength

Peace   that passes understanding

Dissect

Blushes
     Broken
Bruises
     As the
Less than
     Qualified
Less than
     Quantified
Less than
     Cowardly
Lions in the dark game that they play
     In the dark name of the
Less than

You see
     I am a
Less than
     A proud
Less than
     African
Less than
     Savannah cat
That
     Despite the
Less thans
     Have found my way

To rest

    To nest

To broken holiness

    To borderlands

To brotherhoods

    To lesser thans

To sister woods

    To my home sweet home

Despite

    My less thans

Mademoiselle

I've seen the clouds brewing

For years it seems

This bitter pill I've been chewing

Miracles in the making, cause we're an unbreakable team

Coursing through the veins of the dress you're choosing

From black and white souls, no two seconds are free

But what I've known for my whole life is that two blackbirds are cooing

Because what I've known is only you...and me...

Columblind

This   is   for   all   the   suicides

This is for all the   lies

The   sighs

The   cries

The   'whys?'

The why   'me's?'

The dying   trees

The dried   worms

The no   returns

The beauty   flawed

The totaled   cars

These empty   cans

That   understand

Behind this   veil

The dog-less   tails

The honored   guests

The night-less   rests

Those   abused

                                 Used

And   bruised

But above   all...

This   is   for   you

No Name

Pale red, flushed skin of a
brand

new face

Barely

3

So much to look forward to

So little to look

Back

to...

See, her mother left her at the

Bus

stop when she was just a toddler

"Wait here, I'll be right

back..."

she said

But

she wasn't right

back

So the little girl waited on the hard concrete

bench

In the cold

And

breathed

in the inky darkness that surrounded her

Until it drowned her soul

"Be
                              right
back..."
"Be
                              right
back..."
"Be
                              right..."
Her mind was a skipping record
On repeat
Never ceasing
Never sleeping
Ever creeping
Ever weaving
Teeth grinding together
Gnashing like hungry jackals
Tears die in her dreams
Foggy
Soggy
Sloppy, wet sobs woke her
And when she opened her eyes
Everything was the same
The
black
                              was still
black
The far off city lights glowed on the horizon
But

they were so far away

And she was so cold

The small child shivered violently

In fear and frost

Alone and lost

Her eyelids grew heavy

And her head nodded slowly...

Ever so slowly...

To her right

Resting it softly on the frozen

bench

by

the

bus

stop

In the dead night

On the fringes of a city with no name

No one's coming

back

No one will

be

right back

No one's coming to save her

No one will witness as her shivering stops in the cold, sooty
darkness...

Prayz

If you want to see me break into
a thousand pieces, you'll have to wait
I'm whole again, I'm sorry I didn't care the way I should,
instead of love
I gave hate
And now that I'm back to stay I give you my all, I
lay at your feet

Oh, my God,
     D
      a
      d
      d
      y

This is a
                              praise

song for the dead
A coffin
                              nailed

shut, now complete
A cross
                              hung

at my side for so long
This is my
                              praise

    song

Drain the
                                        fluid
from my brain
I'm going
                                        insane
Never in vane
I shall shout your name
Through the
                                        storm
And through the rain
No tempest shall
                                        drain
me
Nothing shall
                                        tame
me
                                Cataract
contacts
                                Invalid
contracts
With demons
In his strength
We will find our way

  Social suicide, get in line, prescriptions are dispensed at the

                        . d . o . t . t . e . d   l . i . n . e .

I am open for
business so m-
ake it the qu-
ickest you ca-
n then die

Tapeworm

In the front of the class
Up until 8th grade
Then as time passed
I got pushed

                        farther

                                    and farther

                                                        back
                                                        Back
of the classroom

                                                        Back
of the line

                                                        Back
of the pubescent wishing well, waiting to be in bloom
Wishing I could go

                                                        Back
in time
To the days when I was picked first
For all the games
Side by side, we'd laugh and play
There was

                                                        no
straight

                        or

                                                        gay
                                                        No
borders

  No

boundaries
                                                        No

brushes
                                                        No

blushes
                                                        No

pimples
                                                        No

scars
                                                        No

good cars
                              Or
bad cars
                                                        No

yesterday
Only today
                                                        No

strait
                                                        No
                                                        gay

See I've never been
                                                        gay

Been straight all my life
But when you wear women's jeans
Life can be
                                                        mean

Bullies can be

                                        cruel
The hurt inside may make you

                                        Hate
your school
May bake your insides
May make you

                                        cry
at night
Maybe you're in the same boat right now
Maybe there's

                                        No-
where to run
So instead of dwelling on the

                                        hurt
Wake up early and look at the sun
Rise in the east
Feel your heartbeat
Feel that?
That's called purpose
With it
You'll make it
Through it all
I promise you all
You'll make it through

Brittle Bones

I feel|closer|to you now that we're
so   far   apart
I pray for you, that you'd fill that lamb-shaped h
                                              o
                                              l
                                              e in your heart
Now that we're so far apart I see all I've done w-
rong
I've
been
pra-
yin-
g f-
or you for so long
And now that I'm strong enough to   stand
                                                     on
                                                     my
                                                     own
I pray you do what's right, I pray that you   learn
                                                     to
                                                     say
                                                     no
We both made mistakes that've turned us into brittle bones
God, bring us back to life, I pray that one day soon we'll both
                                                     learn
                                                     to

say
no

Wimp

The sour note at edge of a symphony
The itch at the brink of eternity
Much of what once was is now gone
I pray that I don't have to wait long

For relief

Sweet release

Of the demons lodged in my cranium
A missile in the dark, pretty and dumb
The bullets of passersby
I take it between the eyes

And I take it to heart

Everything you said, from the end to the start

Suffrage in the slippery wimp I have become
No more assuming the dead never held a shotgun

I'm sorry, I can't write anymore
You've found my weakness, and settled the score...

Steeple

The Tyrants, Never rem-
-ain silent, Yet that's what th-
-ey ask of you, The cZARS, Never co-
-me off as bizarre, Yet they chastise u-
-s for trying not to, The EMperORS, Never s-
-eem to have a temper, As they lovingly twist th-
-eir lies to look so true, The PRESiDENTS, Always sor-
-t out their residents, While we vomit our homelessness o-
-n cardboard, nothing new, This is the world we live in, Wher-
-e the rich binge, And the poor, well...the poor meet a poor end

Lullaby

Lighting a candle to put out the flames

                                            I

drag myself out of the bed that's never been made

It's dark now,

                                            I

never sleep unless

                                            I

'm heavily medicated

Broken bottles, powder prayers, the walking dead are simply sedated

                                                                           She

hides the pills cause

                                            I

can't say no

                                            I

push my foot on the pedal but the car won't go

                                                                         She

emptied the tank and forgot to refill it

But my prescriptions

                                                                         she

has so punctual,

                                            I

find it hard to commit

It's almost like

                                                                         she

likes me in a comatose state

                              I

swear

                              I

'm not making it up, this isn't fake
Cross your heart and swear that you're not trying to overdose me
And maybe

                              I

'll wake up for church tomorrow...we'll wait and see

Please pray for me and my shattered reflection of an existence
Wait a minute, please baby, don't leave, you didn't fill my
prescription

                              I

don't wanna die alone so don't leave me tonight

                              I

self-medicate so

                              I

won't have to remember anything exactly right

It's not what I wanted, it's not what

                              I

need

                              I

light a candle so

                              I

don't have to see anything

                              I

'm alone now, cause

                                                        she
was never real

                                I
just made her up so

                                I
'd have a reason to hate these pills...

Larynx

Stand up and fight
Lemme hear your war cry
Fight till you die
Don't turn or hide

Let your voice be a gun
Shoot down their planes with your words
Let the bullets spray from your tongue
Light up The Enemy's trees and watch them burn

Create a new being out of nothing
Strive
To write
And fight
Paint with a hand grenade
Called your throat

They
won't stop us

They
can't stop us

They
can try

fight

But we will

die

Till we

```
                                                      So
lemme

                                        hear your war cry
Lemme                                   see you stand up
Speak                                                  up
Stick                                                 out
And                                                 shout
                    It    from   the   rooftops
...we              won't          be              stopped
```

Anorexic Insect

They don't care about you-Those fake friends-That eat to binge-
And binge to eat-Your soul-Whole-So what's it gonna be?-Can't
you see?-It's you or me-And it's not gonna be me-That goes down-
Underground-To drown-In the fires of unearthly contact-The

inSECT-That dies-As I shine-Bright-I won't go down without
a fight-So what's it gonna be?-You or me?

Du Jour

Runnin' down the **backstreets** of   **HolyWood**

New **scabs** are peeling, but the **stars** are perfectly content

In their high rise **apartments**, it's all good

But back down in the **alleyways**, **junkie needles** are broken and bent

Just like the bindles, the **homeless children** starve

They try to memorize their thirteenth **script** that'll never get them to the top

Trying to make their dream come true, a **failed "movie star"**

Dope addicts and air **static**, all trying to learn how to stop

Crime pays when **cops** go crooked

Girls younger than you sellin' themselves

Stop me if I'm lying when I say **no**body's good lookin'

And what's up with those **barbie dolls bleached blonde bombshells**?

This is what goes on in are great city of   **HolyWood**

Old **scabs** try to heal, only to be **picked** off before their time

But to everyone else, it's all good

Till they get lost in the **back-ways and trip on a coke** dusted **land mine**

Shhh

In this   void
that I've been   caged
in for so long

I found beauty in the sun's resurrection every dawn

As my failures are laid at your feet

You are the only one that I see

Curse the day and bless this   holy night

                The reverence of my cataract eyes, an unclean sight

                There are stars that never shine for fear of being
outshone

                            My craft, you say, I must

hone

So my tears   s

                                                                       l

                                                                          i

                                                                       t

                                                                          h

                                                                       e

                                                                          r

down the

                                                                       w

                                                                       a

                                                                       l

                                                                       l

                                                                       s

And break open the coming F

                   A

                   L

                   L

So my cares aren't what they once were

I found peace in silence and as the car begins to

                     s

                       w

                         e

                       r

                       v

                      e

The blade is soft

The voice is loud

At what cost?

The   *crucifixion*

of my sound

I don't know why I can't forgive easily

After all, the Creator forgave me

Silhouette

I ret-

urn to my grave every sl-

-eepless night, I fold up between the

cracks, out of sight, My fear engulfs me, My tear-

-set me free, There's a space out there where you and I can

finally decay like fallen leaves, There is a place

somewhere, I know we can find it if th-

-at's what we need, A stran-

-ger's

Silho-

-uette wraps itself around m-

-e, And I feel their fingers brush my s-

-kin, I begin to scream, I return to my grave eve-

-ry pointless day, I fold up in my bed and the inevitable I d-

delay, My fear engulfs me, My tears set me free, T-

-here's a space out there where you and I

-can find refuge, with time we

can f-

-ind

relief, There is a place som-

-ewhere, I know I can fight this anxiety

A stranger's silhouette wraps itself around me, I s-

-hrink against the wall in defeat, This strange silhouette has

a familiar edge, And as I gaze into his eyes I rec-

-ognize with a certainty of my solemn p-

-ledge, These eyes are mine...

Ipecac

M   y eyes have been opened
I see what I've do   ne
My despai   r s   hines brightly
More bright than the su   n

How?
How   could I have hurt you   like this?
Now that I feel your aba   n   donment
Now that I've met sorrow   's   uncaring fist

Broke   n and bloody
My heart lies p   anting on   the floor
Through my   pain the clouds have been lifted
And I know no   w that I've caus   ed anot   her heart to be so
sore

Regret e ats me alive
Consu   ming   me like an ev   er growi   ng fire
Destroying what we had
Out of selfish   and pathetic des   ir   e

So n ow that the fog is lifted
The choice remains
Do I make a stand against what I've   done?
O   r do I stay   the same?

Do I dry my tea   rs and me   n   d a broken heart   ?

50

Or do I flee and begin ane w, a fresh start?

No

I will not surrender

          I wi ll not give up

I will stan d strong, and fix what I've broken asu
nder

Eve n as my heart li es b r oken on the floor

 I k n o w t h e r e ' s a h e a r t o u t t h e r e t h
a t n e e d s m e n d i n g e v e n m o r e

Moth

Goodbye, my

DEAR FRIENDS

I wish we had more time

But it's time for you to leave

To spread your

wings

And slip through the hazy trees

Into the harsh

north winds

Into the foggy beyond

I can't go with you

But I can't bear to see you

fly

Away, but now it's

time to say...goodbye

Goodbye, my dear SOLDIERS

You

fought with all you had

When everyone else gave up hope

You were always there to give a smile to

the sad

Goodbye, my

GO-GETTERS

Goodbye, my HARDHEADED

My SOON WEDDED

Goodbye, my DEAR FIENDS

And leave before I

begin to cry

Goodbye...

goodbye...

52

Inkwife

                                        HAve
yOU EvEr wAntEd tO dIE?
                                        WAntEd
tO crY
                                        WAntEd
tO trY...bUt cOUldn't?
                                        I'vE
bEEn thErE

                                        HAvE
yOU EvEr nEEdEd tO fEEl?
                                        ThE
cOld grIp Of A .22, thE tOUch Of IcY stEEl
                                        AgAInst
yOUr skIn
                                        An
UnExpEctEd grIn
                                        As
YOU swAllOw thE pIlls
                                        AlwAYs
hUngrY fOr AnOthEr nArcOtIc mEAl
                                        ThE
dIlApIdAtEd shIEld
                                        NO
slEEp
                                        FOr

                                                                        53

thE wEAk

                              NO
rElIEf

                              NO
tOngUE And chEEk

                              WEll
I'm hErE tO tEll yOU thAt YOU dOn't hAvE tO blEEd
                              TO
fEEl nEEd

                              ThErE's
sOmOEnE OUt thErE, jUst lIkE YOU
                              WhO
AchEs InsIdE

                              WhO's
hUngrY...jUst lIkE YOU

                              SO
tAkE It frOm mE

                              A
sUrvIvOr

                              A
thrIvEr

                              A
trUth wrItEr

                              It
gEts EAsIEr

                              SOmEtImEs

chEEsIEr

                  BUt

dEfInItElY bEttEr

                  OncE

YOU pUt A pEn tO pApEr

                  And

wrItE thAt fIrst lEttEr

                  SEE

It stArts wIth OnE lEttEr

                  ThEn

YOU Add OnE mOrE

                  SOOn

YOU'vE gOt A wOrd, thEn It blOssOms tO scOrEs

                  Of

wOrds, EAch mOrE bEAUtIfUl thAn thE lAst

                  JUst

lIkE YOUr lIfE

                  YOU

mEEt yOUr wIfE

                  HEr

nAmE Is WrItIng And wIth hEr, YOU mAkE It thrOUgh, YOU hAvE A
blAst

                  SO

dOn't gIvE Up

                  DOn't

gIvE In

                  YOUr

wIfE Is wAItIng

                              FOr

YOUr nEw lIfE tO bEgIn...

Serpentine

```
           |I wasn't r-|
         |-eady to l-|
       |-et go thi-|
    |-s time, W-|
   |-hat's min-|
     |-e has alw-|
       |-ays been -|
         |-mine, Bre-|
           |-ak my nec-|
             |-k for you-|
               |-, you bre-|
                 |-ak my spi-|
                 |-ne, It's -|
                 |-SERPENTIN-|
             |-E...All t-|
             |-his time -|
               |-I waited -|
                 |-for you, -|
                   |-you were -|
                   |-planning -|
                 |-to drag m-|
             |-e into yo-|
             |-ur grave -|
               |-What a mi-|
                 |-stake you-|
               |- have mad-|
```

```
            |-e, It's n-|
               |-ow or nev-|
            |-er, so so-|
          |-rry it en-|
        |-ded with -|
      |-so much h-|
    |-ate, So I-|
  |-'ll end i-|
|-t with th-|
|-e headles-|
  |-s corpse -|
    |-of a snak-|
    |-e, It's S-|
  |-ERPENTINE-|
|-...Releas-|
|-e me, I s-|
  |-cream to -|
    |-the sky a-|
      |-s it star-|
        |-es back, -|
          |-judging m-|
            |-e for my -|
              |-immortal -|
                |-sins agai-|
                |-n, Or jus-|
                |-t kill me-|
              |-, I have -|
            |-been cryi-|
```

```
        |-ng for my-|
       |-self for -|
      |-far too l-|
      |-ong, this-|
     |- story is-|
    |- not for -|
  |-the whole-|
|- family, -|
|-weren't y-|
 |-ou my fri-|
   |end? Relea-|
   |-se me...D-|
     |-rowning i-|
      |-n my own -|
        |-tears, Ha-|
         |-ven't bat-|
        |-hed in we-|
          |-eks, But -|
            |-I found a-|
              |- pair of -|
              |-shears, A-|
            |-lways tho-|
           |-ught I'd -|
          |-have the -|
          |-courage t-|
           |-o speak, -|
             |-Every day-|
               |- I relive-|
```

```
                    |- our time-|
                  |- together-|
                |-, Those b-|
                |-itter win-|
                  |-ter night-|
                    |-s that we-|
                    |- kept eac-|
                  |-h other w-|
                |-arm, Dead-|
              |- images f-|
            |-lash befo-|
          |-re my eye-|
          |-s, foreve-|
        |-r, I wasn-|
      |-'t ready -|
      |-to let go-|
        |-, but you-|
          |- were far-|
          |- too clos-|
        |-e to the -|
      |-other sid-|
      |-e of the -|
        |-storm...I-|
          |- feel the-|
          |- shreddin-|
        |-g whips o-|
      |-f your to-|
    |-ngue agai-|
```

```
|-nst my ba-|
  |-ck, "Merc-|
    |-y" I plea-|
      |-d, but it-|
        |- seems li-|
          |-ke at my -|
            |-pain you -|
              |-laugh...S-|
                |-ERPENTINE-|
                |-...You ha-|
              |-d no idea-|
            |- what you-|
          |- were doi-|
        |-ng to me?-|
          |- The blam-|
            |-e is all -|
              |-mine for -|
                |-falling i-|
                  |-n love th-|
                  |-e first p-|
                |-lace. I s-|
              |-ee that n-|
            |-ow like s-|
          |-trips of -|
            |-film flic-|
              |-kering be-|
                |-fore my f-|
                  |-ace on th-|
```

```
|-e screen.-|
 |- Feeling -|
  |-your warm-|
   |- palm str-|
    |-ike me ac-|
     |-ross the -|
      |-face...Ho-|
       |-w long wi-|
        |-ll this g-|
         |-o on? How-|
          |- long?...-|
           |-Release m-|
            |-e...I wil-|
            |-l be rejo-|
            |-ined with-|
           |- you in t-|
          |-he end...-|
          |-But the e-|
           |-nd is muc-|
            |-h too far-|
             |- for me t-|
             |-o see. Su-|
            |-cking me -|
           |-dry, you -|
          |-are so va-|
         |-mpiric. I-|
        |- can't be-|
       |-lieve thi-|
```

```
                    |-s is over-|
                  |- so sudde-|
                |-nly...Thi-|
              |-s has gon-|
            |-e on way -|
          |-too long.-|
          |- And I'm -|
            |-not that -|
              |-strong. I-|
              |- know you-|
            |- never gi-|
          |-ve me mor-|
          |-e than I -|
            |-can handl-|
              |-e. But I'-|
                |-m smother-|
                |-ed in bla-|
              |-ck, wax c-|
            |-andles...-|
          |-I wasn't -|
        |-ready to -|
      |-let bygon-|
    |-es be byg-|
  |-ones. Wha-|
  |-t's right-|
    |- must nev-|
      |-er be mad-|
      |-e wrong. -|
```

```
            |-Snap my b-|
          |-ack for y-|
        |-ou, you c-|
     |-rack my t-|
     |-houghts. -|
       |-It's sepa-|
         |-rate and -|
           |-it's noth-|
             |-ing but S-|
             |-ERPENTINE-|
           |-...WHY? T-|
         |-here was -|
         |-no eviden-|
           |-ce of the-|
             |- crime to-|
             |- be found-|
           |-. Feel it-|
         |- drip int-|
       |-o pools o-|
     |-f innocen-|
       |-ce on the-|
         |- ground. -|
           |-Punishmen-|
             |-t for my -|
               |-final mom-|
                 |-ents were-|
               |- made int-|
             |-o a sound-|
```

```
        |-. Of a th-|
      |-ousand st-|
    |-amping fe-|
  |-et. To th-|
  |-e beat. O-|
    |-f SERPENT-|
      |-INE. You'-|
      |-re so SER-|
    |-PENTINE. -|
  |-And now, -|
 |-you will -|
 |-never be.-|
|-..mine...-|
```

Sixteen

SHE was just like everybody else

SHE hated every single inch of HERself

With the world that told HER that SHE was a waste of space

Just because SHE wasn't thin enough, tall enough, pretty in pink, SHE wore only black

To hide the fact that HER soul was having a heart attack

Every single second SHE got closer to the end, SHE felt so out of place

i wish someone had said, i wish someone had seen

The worst part of this was that it could have been me

That gave HER a passing glance

Complimented HER smile, gave HER a fighting chance

No the worst part was that i know i could've saved HER

If i stood up and said one word that could've made HER

Feel just like SHE was real

Just like SHE existed

Sad thing is

SHE never thought anyone would've miss it

The day SHE took HER own life, SHE went about HER normal routine

Put makeup on HER face, wear long sleeves

Cut HER wrist a little deeper just so that SHE could breathe

Dried HER tears, did HER makeup again

Didn't want to bring up that SHE didn't have a friend

To HER mom and brother

Who had some much love for HER

Not like the father that was never around

The one that abandoned HER when SHE was only a three-year-old

Packed his bags, turned his back, and then hit the road

Never to return, not a second glance

Never gave HER a kiss, never gave HER a chance

Now SHE's **sixteen**, living life like SHE was a ticking time bomb

It aches me to tell you, SHE thought SHE could never tell HER mom

That secretly inside SHE was overwhelmed and suicidal

Not to mention, that HER mom was HER idol

Went to school that day, never gave a second thought

When SHE reached out for love, SHE drew back HER hand, holding a slipknot

i want it very clear

SHE never thought there was anything wrong from down there

Couldn't see HERself turning paler

As the days became weeks it was apparent there was no inner picture

No happy music, no second glance at a mirror

The only thing SHE saw when SHE looked was a pill bottle growing clearer

The day SHE took HER own life, SHE went to bed early

No one said a thing, not HER mother, not even me

HER only brother

Who could've told HER

SHE meant more to me than any other

See i was only ten, but somehow i knew

Something was very wrong

SHE was so hurt and confused

i'm sorry to tell you this story has no happy ending, no Prince Charming

For that **sixteen**-year-old, who never found it alarming

i remember sitting at the dinner table alone with mom

When my big SISTER took out Daddy's gun from HER bottom drawer and took HER own life

A bang echoed out in a normal house, in a normal neighborhood

When my big SISTER took HER own life

SHE thought SHE'd be doing everyone a favor, by ending it here and now

Instead of holding on just a little longer

i know i could've made a difference if only i was a little stronger...

intermission

I apologize for not explaining this story before Act One began. We've reached the halfway point and you don't even know any of the details. Let's clamber out of this dank theater into the lobby, where it's easier to hear, and I'll catch you up on everything.

Ah, that's much better. Now, as I was writing all the pieces you've read so far, I was beginning to dip into a very thick fog of depression, anxiety, mania, delusion, hopelessness, and despair. My emotions jumped and bumbled this way and that with no apparent rhyme or reason. Some periods I would lay in bed for days drinking in my pain like it was the only oasis in a hundred-mile desert. Other periods I would not sleep for days as if I had engorged myself on pure Methamphetamines. Thus is the reality of Bipolar Disorder.

In my life, everything was crumbling into jagged, needle sharp pieces. I was 22 years old, still living with my parents; unable to keep a job because of my Social Anxiety Disorder, my erratic mood swings caused by my Bipolar Disorder, and my unwillingness to fight my personal demons. I had no income and depended completely on my parent's financial care. I was denied Disability Aid 3 times. The first psychotic break occurred in the middle of that cold summer. On the 10th of June, 2015, I was hospitalized in Brentwood Meadows (a mental facility) for immediate care. There I suffered dozens of anxiety attacks daily. Yet, I survived. Later that year I was hospitalized a second time on the 1st of August. Neither of these double-pronged spurts of hospitalization did me much good. I snarling at the void, and void laughed back.

My friends tried their hardest to support me and help me through the fire, but at the very end of October in 2015, I snapped emotionally and broke all ties to anyone other than my immediate family, who (at the time) I despised.

Looking back, I can clearly see God, Jehovah, Adonai, Alpha & Omega, I Am, Yahweh, Heavenly Father, etc., and his constant guidance and protection. I call him Daddy, but regardless of the name you prefer, it does not change him in the slightest. He was there through the ebony nights and blinding lights. If I had only opened my spiritual eyes, I would have seen him as clearly as you see the words on this page.

Within the 12 months of writing these poems, I attempted suicide 10 times. Twice by a strangulation (the belt snapped both times), once by suffocation by means of carbon monoxide poisoning (the car ran out of gas before I could slip into unconsciousness), once by electrocution (the breaker tripped), and six times by purposeful overdose on Xanax, Ibuprofen (I am deathly allergic to Ibuprofen), and numerous other breeds of pills. These attempts did not fail by coincidence or by naïve methods, mind you.

I lay bare to you, my dear friend, my life in the form of poetry and lyrics spanning a single year. The entire contents of this book were written in approximately 365 days. I'll try to hurry along this explanation of Act One, and I'll give you hints on what to expect in Act Two. I think they're about start, so let's get back to our seats and I'll talk as we go.

Now, on my birthday, the 31st of January, 2016, my ex-girlfriend and one of my closest friends, passed away. I loved Alex, and the loss of her broke my heart as well as my microscopic will to live. For the next several months that followed I planned my final suicide. It would not be an attempt, I refused to not succeed this time. What was the result, you may ask? When you read the poem at the end of this tome entitled Indelible, the answer will be quite clear.

Am I spiritual nut-job? A scripture reading, love screaming, basket case? Probably. I wouldn't be the least bit surprised. But I'm telling you all this because (despite modern American "Christians"), I scream and write truth, love, and hope. I'm here, my friend, to tell you that I am a survivor, as are you if you've tasted death (whether it was intentional or caused by circumstances beyond your control). God has a purpose and a plan for your life and it is your choice to either allow that purpose to come to fulfillment, or to deny him and face this earth alone. I've been tortured by devils and carried by angels, and I've gone through Hell and Heaven. I've chosen which road I will walk, and I know who and what I am.

Look! The curtain is rising. I'm so thrilled you came with me, dear reader. Are you ready to see what the trees hide?

act two:

Ephemeral

Ma(scar)a

Did you

1.)- kiss the ground where she died?

Did you

2.)- place your lips to where she lost her life?

Did you

3.)- feel the concrete where she said goodbye?

...One final breath, deflates her chest, and then she chased the blood out of her veins

Think before you

1.)- Leave it all behind

Think before you

2.)- Close your eyes for the last time

Think before you

3.)- Find out what heaven tastes like

Think before you

4.)- Take the only step you can't justify

Oasis of edges, the blade tip that bites

                    You requested permission for violence

                    -SYSTEM ERROR-

                    .

                    .

                    .

                    .

                    .

                    .

.

.

.

.

Request denied

Mental Floss

k   iD, DON'T YOU PLAY WITH MATCHE   s

t   RUST ME, YOU DON'T WANNA GO UP iN FLAME   s

k   iD, DON'T YOU BREATHE iN ASHE   s

t   RUST iN ME, YOU DON'T WANT THAT KiND OF PAi   n

n   EVER AGAiN, WiLL THE SLUMS BE DENiE   d

n   EVER AGAiN, WiLL i iGNORE YOUR CRiE   s

b   REAK THE GATE   s

i   NFLAMED AND SOR   e

i   'M NOT SAYiNG YOU CANNOT WiN; i'M SAYiNG iT'S GONNA BE HARd

d   ON'T ASK PERMiSSiON TO FiGHT FOR SURViVA   l

t   HE LiGHTS BURNED OUT LONG AG   o

s   O WHY DO YOU HANG AROUN   d?

t   HESE BULBS ARE DEAD AND COL   d

s   O WHY CAN'T YOU JUST LET iT G   o?

i   F YOUR MORALS ARE iFFY, DON'T POST THEM ONLiN   e

t   HERE'S TOO MUCH TALK iN THE WORLD, NOT ENOUGH ACTiO   n

s   AY iT AGAiN, i WON'T TURN FROM YO   u

i   'M HERE, LiKE A BRUiS   e

t   HERE'S MORE TO LiFE THAN THi   s

g   ET iN HiS FACE, AND MAKE HiM PiSSE   d

y   OU'RE STARiNG DEATH iN THE FACE, Ki   d...

s   O STARE HiM DOW   n

76

i   F YOU BACK DOWN, HE WiN   s

i   F YOU BACK DOW   n...

i   N MEMORiAM, MY BROTHERS, LET US STAND STRONG, LET US, STANd

9/19mm

(Sometimes)
the only things left are scars and stains

(Sometimes)
the only motive, leaves the body count the same

(Sometimes)
we can't escape the cage we made, it locks from inside, and...

(Sometimes)
we dig our own grave with the love we display...

(Sometimes)
our pain does not fade away

(Sometimes)
our hate doesn't die the exact same day

(Sometimes)
the friend we love, lost in a club, cannot answer our calls, and...

(Sometimes)
their phones keep ringing; we need to know they're safe...

(Sometimes)
the flags we fly will clash and snag

(Sometimes)
the flags held high, the good and the bad

(Sometimes)
we forget a trigger cannot be un-pulled or forgiven, and...

(Sometimes)
we forget those left alive and the agony left in their hands...

(Sometimes)
late at night, you hear the crinkle of body bags

                                              (Sometimes)
you feel superior and have to remember that an American
                        (Sometimes)
can be responsible for more bloodshed than we can stand, and...
                                              (Sometimes)
their spent clips can be the bedrock for our banner to firmly
stand...

D.S.O.S.

We're

sinking

but

it's

not

the

end

The

waves

kiss...

D.   on't

S.   ave

O.   ur

S.   hip

Ostracize my judgement

Don't

try

to

save

me,

bruising

gently,

I'm

not

drowning,

I'm

just

sinking

Please

don't

fix

me,

tread

in

the

sea,

don't

need

dry

land

beneath

my

feet

I...

am...

meant

to

drift

D. on't...

S. ave...

O.   ur...
S.   hip

Sackcloth

YouinspiresomanypissedoffsongsAlwayssocoy,alwayssocoldYougimmepe
rmissiontostay,solongMaybeit'sallmyfaultTwelvemonthsofHellSometh
ingscan'tbehuggedoutIt'shardtosmile,butheyItjustgivesmemoretocom
plainaboutYouwannacutmeoutIwannacutyoudown[...]You'resobadatbein
gclever,sometimesitstirsupjealousy[...]There'snothingasbeautiful
asbeingisolatedThere'snothingasbeautifulasbeingstuckoutintherain
[...]Ican't...complainCauseI'm...erasedIwon't...createAnexcusefo
rstupidityMaybether'ssomethingwrongwithme[...]Wellyaknowyougivem
ylifemeaningAtleastyoualwaystryIkindafeellikeyoulikeattentionAnd
whynot,why?TwelvemonthsofHellSomewoundsarepickedatlikescabsIgues
sit'sjustaswellSomekidsputknivesinyourbackYouwannacutmeoutIwanna
cutyoudown[...]I'dsaysurvivalisamiracle,somedays[...]Comfortable
inmyownexclusionTherainisn'twhyIcan'tseethesun,I'mtoldTightgripo
nsheetsofpapersolutionsIt'sgivingmetimetoregroupandunfoldTwelvem
onthsofHellI'msovery,verytouchedThecardsays"GetWell"Yourcellopha
nesmileisjusttoomuchYouwannacutme...out[...]Iwon'tmakeanexcusefo
rstupidityMaybethere'ssomething,somethingwrongwithmeYoudon'tneed
anexcuseforstupidityYougotthatcoveredwithoutanyhelpfromme*laugh*

Twinge

Share ~~stars~~, like moth eyelids
Belief can keep me petrified
Tugging heartstrings

Snares and daydreams
~~Spinnerets~~, like burned remains
Wont you, follow me?

Life is a struggle
Worth every strain
Takes every muscle
To keep your head above the waves
Oh, ~~my~~ dear
~~Heaven~~ in your eyes

Empty and left behind
~~Concrete, pantomime~~
Take my hand

Soiled, the aspect
The sub~~arctic~~ complex
I'm not a failure but I do accept applications at this time

There's a way out, the only way out
There's a way out, the only way

Life on my level
Through the blissful decay
Somewhere in a ~~muzzle~~
The ~~voice~~ will never be silenced again
Oh, ~~my~~ dear
~~Heaven~~ in your eyes

~~Feel cold sting~~
A needle inside, a reason to fight
No crook ~~twinge~~
Your eyes wide, deny blind
And I ripped out
Nothing in mine, nothing to hide
Five years since
Blood stained fly, scabbed Valentines

You volunteer my heart
For an auction of sorts
~~Ink in my~~ veins

Breeze ~~bludgeon~~ed skin
Faking every little thing
Painted in me

~~I can't keep screaming~~ to be saved, I've gotta be my own miracle

But...
Life is a ~~push/pull~~

Waves just break

I swear the ~~un~~dertow

Is not gonna win your heart so easily

Oh, my dear

Heaven in your eyes

Life just tangles

Up like a basket case

Past ~~in~~ shambles

No one can turn us into an empty tank

Oh, ~~my~~ dear

~~Heaven~~ in disguise

Please don't worry, ~~all~~ love stories, always ends with someone dying, and

Take my meaning, so misleading, robbing graves to save the living

I'm not leaving, you can't make me, light a match and torch the building

Say you're sorry, please forgive me, ~~well sorry won't erase the memories~~

Stripped, ~~painted~~

No I'm not scared, just feeling despair

Clenched, a ~~pinch~~

No escaping the ~~twinge, the needle slips in~~

Wake up, blacked out

I swear ~~blood work~~, is always worse

Sick, lightheaded

~~Your life is the twinge, let the needle in~~

Collection

<pre>
                                                        A

suicidal fly versus
                                                        a

narcissistic window pane
So close to freedom, you can taste it
                                                        a

million times
With
                                                        a

million different eyes
You can smell the singeing hairs on its body
The ache of countless days under the magnifying lens
The stink of bug
                                                    B.O.,

gagging in his antennae
                                                        &

those wings
Those ashen, useless wings
Buzzing
                                                        &

buzzing
                                                        &

buzzing
But however hard they buzz
They don't get him through that sadistic glass, does it?
You watch him scream at his insectual God in vain
</pre>

you can save him at any point

You can open the window

&

let him die peacefully

You can play savior

But...

Bzzt...bzzt.........bzzt.

(nil)

Why do shrinking walls make me feel safe?
I've been a slave to this bedroom for too long
Drinking in what's behind the stars
Soaking in my own sweat and the sour sting of two weeks straight
I can't fix this by

myself
I can't ask for

help

I finally begin to tell
Myself that the answer is inside
And I need to dig it out
Another foot to the shovel
Another anxiety

attack
Countdown to a

collapse

Here it comes, here it is

I keep seeing purity in my nightmares
Waiting to save me, waiting to stay
Patience is a virtue
Patience is a luxury
That I cannot

afford
Tell me I'm still worth your

time
Please?

Slow clouds work across my ceiling
Slaving away, awake, aware
All my pens are dry
I wrote too much of my unspoken sins on my skin
The only way I can discern the time is the noise coming from

outside,

the heat, the smell of cold air or cut

grass

I'm not sure if you're there or not, but if you are...

Tell me I'm not completely worthless

Tell me there's still hope

Tell me I'm still worth your time

Please?

I'm not asking for a miracle, God

I'm asking for

(nil)

Because

(nil)

is what I know

Hello, My Love

March 29, 2011

Dear Jon,

Hello my love, I've always wanted a pen pal, and I've always loved the art of letter writing, so here goes nothing. I know we've only been together for a short period, but you have no idea how much you mean to me already. You are a very important part of my life. I honestly can't imagine my life without you, and I hope it's something I'll never have to experience. You still give me butterflies, and at this rate I don't think that will ever change. You make me laugh, you make me smile, you make me happy, you make me all warm and fuzzy feeling, you make me a better person, babe. I know I can totally be myself around you. You are everything I've always wanted, and you are all that I need. When I'm around you I feel safe, like nothing can harm me, I know you wouldn't let anything hurt me. You were worth all of the pain and heartache I've gone through, you were worth the search, worth the wait. I hope someday you can see what I see in you, because babe you're simply amazing. I don't see how any girl could have passed you up; I don't see what anyone can see in anyone else but you. I'm sorry you've gone through so much in the past with other girls, but I plan on sticking around for a very long time. You're amazing, Jon, and don't let anyone else tell you any different. You aren't like most people, yes, you're different, and in the best way possible. You are a creative genius, and most of the world just can't understand that. I'm excited to see what God has in store for us, I think only great things lie ahead. Well, I think that's all I got for now.

Love,

Alex

...Dear Alex,

Periodically I get whiffs of your house when I'm out driving,
and the memories come flooding back

I hear you singing along to a song playing on the radio, even
though you always hated your voice

You would sing the words quietly and hope I can't hear...but I
can

Over the winter winds screaming outside the car, over the
grumble of the engine, I hear your soft, soft whisper lyrics

You never miss a beat or a word

And in awe I sit

And listen

Wondering if you'll make any mistakes...but you never do...

I snap back to reality and it's just me

Alone in my car

And it seems just a few degrees colder than it was a second ago

I feel your hand squeezing mine tightly when I go over a bridge,
those scratchy wool fingerless gloves that you always loved to
wear up against my slender, naked hands as we tackled the mighty
Ohio together

On our way to Henderson

We both have a huge fear of heights, and bridges, so we just
hold on tight as the CLUNK CLUNK CLUNK of the tires hitting the
grooves in the concrete fills our senses

But we made it

Every single time we made it...

I snap back to reality and I'm driving to band practice

I'm alone in the car

And I'm going over a bridge without you...

I taste your grilled cheese sandwich when I bite into my own attempt at grilled cheese...I can't remember how you made them, so mine are always horrible...they just don't stand a chance

You just made me one because (despite my constant insisting that I'm fine, you somehow knew that I hadn't eaten that day)

You wouldn't let us leave for church until I had eaten

And promptly taught me the "right way" to make grilled cheese

I devoured that thing while you sat next to me in that old, old timey kitchen, grinning ear to ear as I ate

When I finished, you kissed my cheek, dropped my plate in the sink and said "NOW we can go"

I drift back now and it's late at night

I'm in my own kitchen, chewing on greasy toast

And you didn't make this...

I made this

I throw away my almost completely uneaten food and go back to bed

And at night, I close my eyes and I'm looking down at you as you lay in that casket

In your favorite dress

I'm in this numb trance, but I notice your face

They put all the wrong makeup on you

You don't look like you at all

And I get angry

I mean really, really angry

But then I notice the tattoo on your arm

The one I always knew, and there was no denying that this was you

I smiled a little and whispered the words that are still there, even though you aren't...

"Above all else, never forget to love"

As I walk away, a single, sentimental tears slides down my face

We never did, did we?

We never forgot to love...

<u>Empty Vessels</u>

        smell
I can   the fake flowers of   soaked into stale breath
                          detergent

It's almost like I'm really here
Like she's really here
Like we never left at all
But the truth
          honest to God truth
The real,

Is whatever you might see
        beating   breathing   that you perceive

Whatever   and   **vessels**

Are **empty**

Blistered and withered
Shivering in the dark
Two inches tall

Tiny little thumbnail **vessels**

Both, side by side
Neither alive
Neither quiet dead

Tasting each other's nectar

love fueled hate crime

In the aftermath of a

empty vessels

See, we, you, me these   that can't
quite breathe

That can't quite

          see

Can't quite

      Believe

                 inky

That there's anything other than each other in the   void

She tells me to **ex**plore

She tells me to abandon her

To leave this tundra and push forward into the ebony desert

To look for someone that might fill me

That might take off my lid and pour liquid into my shell

Someone to change me into a

                  container

But...

It's just her and me here

And if I leave her...I'll never find her again...

So here we

                    sit
    Idiotism

                                                    incarnate,

    ignoring our father's advice
    Ignoring as our souls cry
    Ignoring as we softly die
    Ignoring each other's sighs
    Two microscopic bottles
    Dry as a bone
    Alone
    With each other and no one else
    In the cold
    In some remote desolation of our own creation
    Somewhere

    Two **empty vessels** gather dust...

Ascension

I will claw

I will crawl

I will ball

Up my fists around the roots

And pull

My

Way

Up

This craggy

Crackling

Cauldron of confusion

And broken bodies

Moaning

Loaning

Groaning

But

They

Stay

Still

But not I...

I will continue to climb

To ride

To rise

I will not hide

I will not shied

Away from crawling upward

99

Through the dents

Through the vents

From the crevice

In the depths of the ocean

To peel the sun's skin

Blistered and burned

Scorched and scourged

I continue my ascent

Into paradise

Where my demons will fear my name

And I will know theirs

I will fight

I will rise

I will claw

And crawl

In the dust

And mud

And in the sand

I will make my stand

Right here

Right now

I will not look back

Will not turn from the attack

I will climb this mountain

Because the alternative...

Is to fall back

To crawl back

Into the cave where I came from

The blackest pit of existence I have ever known

The cell bars there, carved from human bone

Lost lives

And shattered souls

Hopeless creatures slowly waiting to heal their wounds

An early tomb

I won't

I refuse

And

I

Will

Continue to climb

Yes

Until my time...

I

Will

Climb

Honeycomb Lungs

Breathing through honeycomb lungs

Tugging and struggling to crawl our way home

Sickened and sedated

Defeated and deflated

Sucking air into those soggy hives

Finding there's no excuse for not feeling alive

See we all have excuses

We all have reasons why

We can't get up to say goodbye

We all have our questions

We're guilty of wanting to try

But when it comes down to it, we all just wanna live to die

To be let out of our cage

A walk to the edge

To stare down over the lip

Peer past dunes of what we said

The dogs are left hungry

Storm front overhead

The bills are unopened

Can't crawl outta bed

Sometimes you can't sleep at all, your skull full of self-accusations

The red flags are there

But we don't care

Cause sometimes sadness is a warm blanket

Other times we sleep far   too much, but how can we   defend our
act   ions   ?

When that voi   ce in your b   rain

Begs for relief   of the pai   n

There's no e   asy, three ste   p program to co   mplete sati
sfaction

I was asked to descry   be dep   ression, is it really as   bad as
it seems   ?

I smiled and s   aid...

" E v e r y o n e   h a s   a i r   i n   t h e i r   l u n g s
b u t   n o t   e v e r y o n e   c a n   b r e a t h e "

Daddy

I close my eyes

I'm w a l k i n g

And everything is snow

Too white

Too bright

I'm waiting to fall through this haze

And wake up, drenched in sweat

But I don't

I'm pushing f o r w a r d

It's scary to be the only smudge on the canvas

But I can't get this feeling out of my head

That maybe it's going to be alright this time

So I w a l k

And w a l k

And w a d e

Through a river of *diamond eyes*

I'm waiting to wake up

Cause I feel **too** good for this to be real

This must be the best dream I've ever had

But you have to wake up sometime

You have to swim back to reality, right?

This is a high I never want to lose

I refuse

To *sober* up

To ~~cover~~ up

To give up this euphoria just because I don't feel worthy

Just when I start losing hope

When I don't know where to go

What to do

I see a smudge like myself, but a smudge so much lighter than the surrounding page

As it a p p r o a c h e s, and I a p p r o a c h it, I'm overwhelmed once again

I know this smudge, I know him

I've never seen him face to face, but I couldn't confuse him with anything or anyone else

I saw his   eyes,

and then I was in the most gentle bear hug between father and son

My eyes started to sting and I tried to say a lifetime of lost **words** but my mouth

My mind

My tongue

My being, was dumb

I had nothing, no words to express

So just held him tight

I held on for dear life with my daddy

For a long time, WE   stood and embraced, softly crying through the **bliss**

My lips parted and I whispered "I've been waiting **87 years** to hold you..."

There was a moment of silence but then he finally responded "For **87 years** I've been holding you..."

Afterwards:

My eyes are pouring out tears

Fat, choking sobs escape as I watch my best friend lay on a

        wooden board,
        covered in bruises,
        blood pouring out of him from a million openings

that I caused...
I'm horrified as I see a

        nail gun pushed up against his wrist

and when it does I scream
He looks me in the eyes
And through more torture than any best friend can take he says
in short gasps

        "It's going to be okay. It's okay.
        It's okay. I **promise** it's going to be..."

But that's as far he goes because

        they pull the *trigger* on the **nail gun**

He

        Screams

They do it

again

He screams louder

They punch a **nail**

a third time through his body

and then they hang him up to die

For what I did

Not him

Me

I'm lying in the dirt and sand

Crying for him

He keeps

CALLING my name and comforting me

"It's going to be okay.

It's going to be okay. It's okay.

I forgive you. It's gonna be...

alright..."

Marie

You are more **beautiful** than you ever will

Know.

Problem is not that you hate the

cold,

it's that you only see

snow.

See, I see the frost blooming in your eyes and I

know,

even if you

don't...

You are **beautiful.**
Not glossy and

fake

Not airbrushed or foundation

caked

No,

YOU are a breathing

canvas

And I'm watching the artist paint a

masterpiece

It's such a pity you don't

see

the detail and brush strokes,
the **real**ism,
the contrast,
the texture,
the creation
...that is you.
And I wish you wouldn't look at your own

reflection

In a shattered mirror, just to assume

rejection

      Is the

direction

    you were meant to take...
      See, your

obsession

      with

perception

    is unhealthy and it's a

deception

    that evolves to

inflection,

  which in turn leads you right back to a flawed

reflection

    and assumed

rejection.

This vicious cycle continues to rip apart your

soul

And it seems like there's only one way to make you

whole

To gather your heart, piece by piece

Thecrackedfragmentsofyou,leftscatteredonthepavementlikeacarwindo
w'sfailedencounter...with a light pole.

And when we have your heart,

tattered

and

shattered

Just like the mirror who said **YOU** don't

matter

We'll get the best pieces and glue them

together

It doesn't look bad compared to the

latter

And the

art

we made out of a broken

heart

Reminded you of something your mom use to

say...

right before she passed

away.

"Never forget that each snowflake is **unique**, and each snowfall
can be gone in a

day.

Embrace the

cold

And never

unfold

Unless your petals are here to

stay

I love you

Marie

And you love

me

And that's what matters at the end of the

day

A broken

                                        reflection

can be fixed with

                                        perception

If the

perception

...is a smile on your face."

20cc

Whisper,
         whisper in my ear
Tell me what you need,
                      my dear

Touch my...adulthood
I'm waiting...

I'm lowering you
               down
Rope's taut, raw dust and rusted
                      saw
I'm passing you
                  'round
Gut feeling, I'm a
                                                    20cc

survivor
         Fighter
You're a
                                                    20cc

debater,
         hater
No escaping a troubled
               undertaker

I'm painting in blood above my

door

Praying you'll show love and pass us
    o'er

Mumbling in

riddles

Screaming in

Psalms

Drowning in

    puddles

A calm before the

    napalm

Father, am I lost?

Father, am I found?

Father, never question your

creator

I guess I'll always be a

20cc

    taker

Whisper in my

ear

Tell me what I wanna

   hear

Sister, sister, forgive my

    tears

The needle broke, but I'm still

    here

Pearl

A silken web

Like spider eggs

I slept upside-down

My hair brushed the ground

A jaded thread

Dead family pet

My veins keep collapsing

My brain keeps relapsing

I'm anti-suicide

But I'm sure as Hell not lovin' life

Tomorrow   seemed   pretty,   yesterday
Now   it's   here,   just   take   it   away

Hand her a gun, she'll rule the w-
orld, Hand her a gun, depraved, H-
and her a gun, fill it with pearl-
s, She's gonna make us...all obey.

A human hair

Like swollen prayers

John Doe, early 30's

Removed all prints and teeth

A dress tears

Like all your dreams

An insectual night

With an overweight fly

I'm an anti-cutter

But that doesn't mean I hate razors

I know there's a God that never strays
If I feel alone then who walked away?

A virgin's kid
  Like burlap stitch
 I crawled under the porch
         To save any remorse
                A loving slit
             Like dried pen ink
          I cannot surrender my lips
              Even if it's just one kiss
                   I'm anti-Anti-Christ
            But my sins were fun to commit, I can't deny

Save us from this monster I created

A silken web
Like spider...eggs

Bulletproof

I like to think of myself as   strong

Seems now I was dreadfully   wrong

Thanks for the gun shells in my   chest

Erase every thought, just   exist

This,

truth,

you,

use;

is,

not,

abuse

This,

is,

tough,

love;

it's,

not,

enough

Failed them   again

Looks like they   win...

I look so   malnourished and pale

That's what you say as you   derail

My train of   "thought and of hope"

Shivering in the   bitter cold

I'm,

not,

bullet,

proof;

I'm

just,

confused

Do,

I,

look,

fine;

when,

I,

flat-,

line?

Hurt my feelings

I must be empty...

Dear God, do I look alright to   you?

I'm not   bulletproof

Slapping Band-Aids on a bullet   wound

I'm not   bulletproof

Feeling it   out

That's enough   now

I gave it a   try

Now where do I   sign?

I once thought of myself as a   man

But I can't be what society   demands

I tried for years to keep   calm

But now I'm done playing   along

You,

can,

fill,

me;

full,

of,

lead,

please

I,

can't,

deny;

your,

app-

e-

tite

Dying before   combat

That's really too   bad...

Dear God, do I look alright to   you?

I'm not   bulletproof

Slapping Band-Aids on a bullet   wound

I'm not   bulletproof

Never been, never   will

I'm not   bulletproof

Never been,   empty/filled

Looks like they   win...

Nicotine

Bruises spinning like marionettes
Twirling on cold strings in my head
Bruises from a loving hand
Something I'll never understand

Falsetto daydreams
Inflamed and dirty
These things we gotta get off our chest
Jim Jones' Kool-Aid
Preconceived beauty
These things that never really exist

Confessional

I dissect the thought of you into a million pieces
I rejected the memories that snaps like dirty needles
I'm not alone

Gimme one last comforting smile
You're fading fast and I know
You won't be here forever
It's like you're gonna disappear
Even though you're still here
It's now or never
Forget anything but my love
My face, my name, I'm you're son
You won't know me in the morning
God, take anything that you want
My heart, my mind, and my lungs
Just don't take away...
My mom

Don't take her away from me

I've, become so cold
I just unfold
She's slowly slipping away
Like, she's just died
In her mind
She doesn't know my face

The one, that always cared

Times we shared

We used to laugh, now we just stare

Erupt, I've had enough

Stunned and numb

I can't save you from this monster inside your tears

This was her confessional

Even her sins sounded beautiful

Must've been tough as Hell

To say "Son, I'm losing myself'

This was her confessional

Her baby sins seemed so pitiful

Must've been so terrible

To have to tell me "It's time for me to go"

Mote

A
  tiny
     hole
        A
         pinprick
Almost
      invisible
           to
            the
               naked
                  eye
Yet
   what
      pokes
         through
Is
   a
   microscopic
         thread
            of
              light
A
  bronze
      bridge
Between
     the

                    black

                         cold

                            and

                               the

                                  bright

                                     color
An

   island

          in

             the

                sea

                   of

                      eyeless

                            dark

                                  waves

                                     and

                                        caressing,

                                               clammy

                                                    hands
This

     hole

          is

             home
This

     hole

          is

             holy
This

hole,
    makes
      me
       whole
The
  mistakes
    I've
     made
The
  macramé
The
  empty
   dinner
    plate
Is
 a
  reflection
    of
     this
      cave
In
 a
  wispy
   veil
She
  shines
   through
One

```
        place
One
    point
Hope
      in
         this
              world
                    of
                       gnarled,
                              diseased
                                      limbs
Lanky
       with
             deformation
Dilapidated
               and
                  deflated
A
  desert
A
  black
        hole
A
  void
But
     still,
            it
               pokes
```

                    through
Ever
      shining
Ever
      burning
Lighting
          one
              candle
                    to
                      desecrate
                              the
                                  dark
I
  crawl
        towards
                that
                    pinprick
With
      hope
          in
            my
              heart,
                    mind,
                          soul,
                                and
                                    reflecting
                                            in
                                                my

  pale

                                                        eyes

There

        is

            hope

I

    find

        my

            salvation

                    in

                        that

                            mote

                                of

                                dusty

                                    light

In

    the

        promise

                    of

                        beauty

                            reaching

                                out

                                    to

                                    me

                                        with

                                            both

                                                hands

Precious

              sliver
Take
    me
        into
            your
                arms
And
    remind
            me
There
        is
          a
            hole
                in
                    the
                        void
And
    it
      is
        worth
            every
                drop
                    of
                        sweat
                            in
                                my
                                    body
                                        just

to

  reach

     it

Apartment 2B

Police sirens were my lu-
llabies. I couldn't slee-
p until they went by. Th-
e blue and red, my night-
light. Yeah, that's who -
tucked me in at night.

The shots they popped of-
f near me. We're my only-
bedtime stories. The mor-
als of trigger finger po-
lice. Goodnight, sleep t-
ight, rest in peace...

Pseudophile

rose tide the before remember I

Inside

pseudophile no You're

time of blink a than more You're

this allow can't You

away Lap

throat your at is edge the Till

undertow the feel never You

this enjoy can't You

life my In

alone all swim to Set

souls broken many too seen I've

this condone can't I

times our Of

fallacy a ,tomorrow of promise The

casualties many too far been There's

this accept can't I

Lip

When.your.body.won't.stop.shaking

And.your.heart.won't.stop.breaking

When.your.world.falls.apart,.let.your.knees.hit.the.ground

If.all.you.have.are.demons

And.you've.lost.all.your.reasons

If.you.need.a.miracle,.a.pair.of.lips.won't.let.you.drown

Come.to.me.through.this.catastrophe

I.will.be.everything.you.could.ever.need

Come.to.me.and.try.to.believe

I.will.show.you.how...to.kiss.the.demons.out

Come.to.me.through.your.agony

I.will.redeem.all.your.years.of.suffering

Come.to.me.and.I'll.set.you.free

I.will.show.you.how...to.kiss.the.demons.out

Lukewarm

Another day
          s
           l
           i
            t
             h
              e
             r
           s

            softly by
And I still can't look you in the **eye**
I fight the **tears** that refuse to die
I watch as an ANGEL
            glides
            past
            my
            side

I dream of you when I'm w   i   d   e awake
You're so BEAUTIFUL, and I'm so irate
You don't even know my **name**
And I'm the only one I can blame
You're a creature of **PERFECT**ION and GRACE
But I'm an insect staring at you, in my disgrace

Yeah, you're the girl who doesn't call me **gay**

But I'm just the school **fag**, always in last place

                          a h a e
I'm tired of the b t w t r being lukewarm
I need you to see me, see me at all

    soft **sapphire** in your
This   gaze
  see you through the curtain of my
I   hair
    you're looking right at
And   me
  stumble to my
I   chair
    sit across from me, like every
You   day
    this time you stop and stare, almost in
But   **awe**
    stammer, take a moment to
You   breathe
    say "Hi
And   **Jon...**"

Maternal

Skitter, scatter
Across the dull linoleum
Claws and nails clicking
Clacking, louder than life knives leaving scratches and canyons in the plastic foliage

They smell fear
Wafting on a wave of irritated heartbeats
Olphactory hairs quiver and twitch
Shiver and twist
Writhing in the sea of odor that beacons them to come and drink
Calls to them, like sirens to sailors

Pleads with them
Begs them
Surrenders all just to draw them towards the source of the smell

A small child
Absorbed in violence
Hungry ghosts clawing in her stomach

They scurry closer
Following the road signs of smell and sound
Taking in the predatorial instinct of a million years
And indulging in its foamy down
Specks of spittle are lost as they go in for the kill
Daggers out

Teeth bared

Hackles raised

    This is it

This is the gluttonous feast

    This child will be digested for a thousand years

They can taste her on their tongue

                    This...

              is...

        it...

But...

    The sun snaps awake, flooding the kitchen with florescent glow, burning their eyes

The screams of these demonic wall dwellers pierce the cold quiet

    They wail and beg for mercy against the unforgiving light

Begging for mercy that they would never show for the child

                  Hair shrivels and smokes

Fangs clatter out of their gaping mouths onto the shiny kitchen floor

    Their eyes wither

Their tails curl up like strips of fat on an open flame

    Subterranean evil crawls back into holes in the walls, leaving behind a trail of melted tar and nicotine stains

                  The child's tear-stained
              face rises

A microscopic smile plays on her face

    Mother is home

And what, I ask, is better than that?

Screwdriver

What if

the roles were reversed?

What if

a heterosexual man was condemned to Hell for loving a woman?

And the reason they're love is an abomiNATION is because homosexuals misinterpreted their beloved doctrine?

What if

a man married a man, or if a woman married a woman, God would bless the union

However, the pagan belief that a man could be joined (in church and in law) with a woman in holy matrimony, was...unheard of?

What if

your sexuality was taboo?

What if

how you were born was payable by death?

What if

the fact that you are strait meant that you were not entitled to equal rights...how would you feel?

I ask you, my friend

What if

the roles were reversed?

<u>**People, Places, Progress & Pews**</u>

                                        Is this what progress is?

Men beaten to death

Women raped and tortured

Children (sold)iers

Mass executions as cinder blocks rain

In Jesus Christ's holy name

We avert our eyes from

                                        Darfur

                                        Sudan

                                        Rwanda

                                        Nicaragua

                                        ...New Guinea

Genocidal

    Homicidal

        Suicidal

           Sitting idle

As religion

    Race

        Disagreements

           Political upheaval

           Saint-ish evil

And any other excuse we can think up is taking the lives of
hundreds of thousands, nay, millions...as we speak

                                        Is this what progress is?

When we, as Amer-I-Cans

Chosen caretakers of this world

141

Given by God AND by guns

    Can sit on our couch

        Our porch

            Our car seat

                And declare in

ONE...MIGHTY...VOICE...

..."It doesn't affect us"...

Why should lives matter if we don't know them, right?

As long as we meet our quotient and go to church on Sunday

As long as our right to bear arms

Our favorite pew

Our "we don't care" attitude

Is still our God given right...then our ticket to heaven is free

Checked and stamped

Waiting (at our convenience) at the closest local McDonald's drive-thru window

Would you like to SUPER-SIZE that Anti-Christ Big Mac?

                        Is this what progress is?

I watched a man being bound

    Shoved to the ground

        Beaten

          Stabbed

            Beaten once more before being murdered when a concrete block was dropped on his head...

Oh yes, **we are angry**

We are angry

because work wasn't comfortable

We are angry

because we have to move one of our cars to let someone else in the driveway

We are angry

because someone else is using the bathroom and we need to take a shower before work and we're already late because...we slept in

We are angry

because the TV isn't working perfectly

We are angry

because all we have to eat is a refrigerator full of food that doesn't sound good right now (thank you very much)

Is this what progress is?

When the teachings of

Love

Compassion

Acceptance

And salvation

Is made into an excuse to commit a genocide

When we turn our heads

And close our eyes

When someone tries to upset our fragile constitutions with news that there's more than just America on this planet, we put our fingers in our ears and scream

"LALALA-I-CAN'T-HEAR-YOU-LALALA!"

After all the scientific achievements from the

    Omnipotent

        All seeing

           All hearing

             All knowing people

that we perceive ourselves to be, we still find ourselves in this state of

"We'll learn to swim when the flood gets to our necks" mentality...we have to ask ourselves...

            ...Is this what progress is?

Paper, Not Skin

Alone at last,
just you and   I
It's been too long,
how have you been?
     I just broke up with Suicide
I hope she understands
that we can't stay friends
There's a fine   line
     between razors and pens
But just for   tonight let's choose paper, not skin
Yeah just for   tonight...

I know you
loved her with all your heart
I know you
wanted to fix her   broken
                wings
But you know she's too afraid to fly, and it's too
               dark
To make any decisions that requires
          suffering

<u>I</u>

...hey babe, im sad. write something about me? plz? <3
3:22 A.M.

i 4got my fire when i set U ablaze, i 4got
my own desires when i met Ur gaze, & i don
't need 2 shine anymore, cuz i just lit up
a rainstorm. i surrendered my life when i
saw Ur lite, i surrendered my disguise whe
n U held me tite, no, i don't need 2 hide
anymore, cuz i just lit up a rainstorm.

This is my life, this is control, i surren
der it all, just hear U call, my name, it'
s like cocaine, watch the fire rain. This
is my time, this is my soul, i surrender i
t all, just 2 hear U call, my name, the cl
ouds n flames, watch the fire rain.

Where r the signs, that something's not ri
te? My back feels fine, cuz there's been n
o knife, i can't b scared anymore, cuz i j
ust lit up a rainstorm. U started as a spa
rk, got a flicker in Ur eyes, nothing like
a heart, 2 remind U ur alive, i can't pla
y dead anymore, cuz i just lit up a rainst
orm.

i need something tangible, something concr
ete, i need something pliable, that won't
break my feet, when i land, oh, take my ha
nd...here goes nothing.

BURN! i wanna c the sky's seams be torn, c
uz i just lit up a rainstorm, BURN! the pa
in melts away, watch the fire rain.

3:46 A.M.

<u>Jenesis</u>

I woke up

face down on the bathroom floor

And, someone was yelling   and pounding on the door

Everything was sliding to the left

and right on their own accord,

the world was spinning, but I wasn't...

I looked over and there was an open ~~pill bottle~~ staring at me, accusing me

It was empty

It's previous inhabitants were evicted and forced to move into my stomach...

all ~~30~~ of them

My throat was raw and I couldn't stop the

pounding on the door, the voice asking if   I'm okay

...I crawled on all fours to the door and unlocked it

Someone said

"oh my **God**"

...I think...

If they were screaming at one end of a tunnel, I was on the other side, only hearing the echoes and the far off white static that buzzed like a livid Mud ~~Dauber~~

I don't know what's going on

but I'm pretty sure I just   downed a whole bottle of "~~pain~~" ~~killers~~

It's getting hard to

                                        breathe

but I'm starting to go

numb

...Not that it matters, but

this ~~anti~~-high is terrifying

...right before I blacked out I heard my   mom   whisper

                    "...I told you he'd do

                    this...

                    don't say we didn't

                    warn you..."

Evermore

The lights are on   but no one's home

I'm too scared   to   face myself

                                                  alone

Maybe it's just me,   this is getting old

Every night smothered   in the   cold

Smoking   *propaganda*

Light   'er   up

I crawl   beneath   your skin

So I don't have   to feel the love

Groaning bones   givin'   in

But we   crawl   over them

I survive for   you, my   friend

Cause I   can't   die again

Don't you dare   shine   without your

                    scars

There's nothing worse   than   a perfect

                    star

Nail gun on her   wrist, a lamb's **womb**

Take comfort, empty   lies the   tomb

How long will   this

                                        last, dear **Lord**?

Quote the   demon   *"evermore"*

Mental illness,   restraints,   and

```
                                        pills
Depression, anxiety,                social  spills
Think for yourself          and push the
     limits
Never assume life           is a
     given


Taming your hate            without a    gun
I'll take you         down using my tongue
Get up, you have a          voice, you have a      choice
You have the                            noise,
          now go                        destroy


What's left besides the          lies              and


The Enemy's


burlap              horns?
The comfort that         nothing lasts


evermore
```

Endcantations

Raging
        harmonic ~~crescendos~~
Taking
        in my fallen heroes
Parachutes for Holocausts   .
                (or hollow-costs?)
A pack
        of the lost
Faces
        in a magazine
So airbrushed and so   pristine
No   flaws,
no   scars,   God forbid
We glorify difference

                                        Father, have we been
                                led astray?
                                        Father, have I lost my
                                way?
                                        Father, it feels like
                                I'll be alright

I can finally breathe tonight

Souls buried   alive
  in a casket
                Self-pity

is a

warm blanket

Feels so good to live in   pain

Till pain evolves to   suffering

            At the scene of the crime

            No soul will dare deny

            I didn't bat an eye

            I watched with glee, when my love made The Devil

commit suicide

If I Die Tonight

_MY

   room makes such a good   tourniquet

   When

_mY

   thoughts bleed on tissue paper

_MY

   bed can't give me the   same fix

   I just don't want to remember

   Cold is the   soul that refuses to love

   In the dark, who can know?

   I know I need to   fight

   But it just doesn't feel   right

   I can't

_{den}Y

   the   cold

                    If I die tonight

   , please just let me know

_MY

154

pain is

Temporar**y**

    It can't last **if**

    I survive

    If I can't fight for me

    I'll fight for

    You

    Tell me it

    Will be just fine

    Even **if** its

    Just a   lie

    Tell me it'll be alright

    Please don't

cr**y**

<u>If I die tonight</u>

    Don't

cr**y**

    In

Your

    arms

    Hold me through this

Don't leave me
Alone   like   she   did
The calm before
Before the storm
Is a heart not
Not

Y_{et}

    torn
If I don't fight for
Me, I'll fight for

Y_{ou}

If I survive
I live for

Y_{ou}

Look me in the

          e Y es,

friend
It's gonna hurt
Hope through pain
Life   in rebirth

Suffocate
The razor   blade

In trash, I wanna   watch it fade
Under page
Upon page that surrenders me
I can't STAND around and watch

You

bleed

Kill self-image
Kill fake hearts

You

can't shine
Without a spark

MY

last request
Light up the dark

You

don't
know how precious

You

are

Flatline

I left before you were ready
You didn't kiss me goodbye
I felt your lips cold and empty
Pressed yours against mine
I left you too soon, please trust
I promise my intentions were pure
I'm not here to hold you up
But you can swim, I'm sure
Can't fill my grave with flowers
My body is the only thing it'll take
I can't show you the hours
I spent weaving you a hiding place
So that when I left you alone
You'd have an escape
From this world of headstones
We'll be together, one day

Remember that night
We lay under the stars
With tears in your eyes
Feel the beating of my heart
That beauty will never fade
I won't forget those times
When I held you in the rain
There was nowhere left to hide
We found comfort in each other

158

Till the clouds drifted   away
    Only   then   could   we   discover
It didn't matter what we   say
    What   mattered   were   your   tears
What mattered was my   heart
    What   mattered   was   that   you   were   near
When everything fell   apart

    These   stairs   I   take
Each one   caress
    The   ~~life~~   I   hate
The ~~life~~ I   _miss_
    If   you   could   hear   me
Would you hold me   tight?
    Until   I   fell   asleep
Until you doused the   lights
    In   the   growing   darkness
You know you're not   _alone_
    You   can   smell   my   fragrance
In the fibers of your   clothes
    I   couldn't   take   very   much
I need what I _abandoned_   now
    But   I   didn't   think   of   that   when
    I   stepped   off   the   edge   and   let
    you   all   down

don't say goodbye, don't fade into the night, don't leave my side, until I flat line

Tapeworm

There's a **heartbroken** six-year-old that lives in that house
at the end of the block

See him?

On the concrete step

Right outside the front door...

He's maybe twenty pounds **underweight**

Sandy blonde hair

No shirt

No shoes

Just black Wal-Mart shorts that have to be two sizes too big

Twiggy arms and ribcage blatantly exposed like some seductive
prostitute showing more skin to get more clientele...

But there is   nothing immoral,

             nothing sexual,

             nothing tempting

or arousing about seeing a

     starving child,

     half naked,

     baking in the June summer oven

There's yelling coming from inside the house...

              "YOU SLEPT WITH WHO?"

                        "I gotta pay for yer cigarettes,
                        don't I?

"Gotta pay fer the car

"The rent

"The insurance

"The electric's out
already...

"Behind on gas...

"...Had ta"

...There's a crash

More yelling...

The boy chokes back a sob but it bursts out regardless...

And we drive by

We roll the windows up and turn on the AC

It's none of our business

It's none of our concern

Our world will keep turning

While his falls apart...

"Had ta

No choice

No money

"...Had ta"

Bleach

MY heart is covered in paper cuts

MY Valentine's card is covered in blood

MY crime scene is covered in love

MY church pew is covered in disgust

MY rearview is covered in compassion

MY headlights are covered in mud

MY words are covered in actions

MY secret hate will be judged...

Taxidermy

Specks of ebony flotsam
Perverting the glass like some
Serial killer crime scene photo

Nursery for a giant insect
Cartoon candles fling their
Articles of uncertainty

On the floor
On the walls
The ceiling
The door handles
The frames
The drapes
The fire escape
The bed

Basking in the 'don't tell me what to do'
Attitude

A hotel room full of static
White noise and dead silence
The tee-vee, black
The f-own, unplugged

Feed m-eye mind

Nourish m-eye   ghost

Eye want to learn to   question everything

Until eye know them   face to face

Tongue to   tongue

Intimacy   of a soulmate

Tree   bones

Pen tattoos gently caressed into the bodies of   leaves

Bound   together

F   O   R   E   V   E   R

Empires   fall

Kings   die

Democracy   burns

But   beauty

I   S

F   O   R   E   V   E   R

Ingrate

Is it okay if I be strait with yo   u   ?
There are days when I don't know   w   hat to do
Times when it feels like a   n

                                      o

                             o   s

                                e

Is choking   ME
     The   pressure   really gets to ME
     I don't fit in, I cannot please
     Just once it would be nice to breathe

     I hope you don't mind my **honesty**
But if anyone asks...

                    I'm just fine
                    I'm alright
            Things couldn't be better
            Cause life is just so grand
                    I'm just peachy
                    There's nothing wrong at all
                    If I complain
                    I'll be back against the wall
                         So today...
                    I'm okay

Just fell apart in class   today

166

It was funny to everyone but ME

I'm bawling in a stall to   **escape**

Found solace 'cause the *ugly*   **pray**

These cluttered halls, with empty

        minds

   That can't

                smell a soul that just died

Hopefully they'll get a

              whiff of flies

      I'm not a

rotten INGRATE

      But I am

rottin' IN a GRATE

Gurney

          high rise
On a
          suicide
Teen
               tired
Aren't you
                lie?
Of living a

                again
Depression
            in
Slipping
                awake
I swear I'm
          resurrection
I need

                                        Stone rolled away from the tomb
                                                  Still we refuse
                              Wish the overdosing
          Could never consume
                                                  Raging addictions
                                                  Laid at your
feet
I didn't have a problem until I woke up on a gurney

```
I

                              NEED

 a constant voice
A long dead reverence


I

                              NEED

 a reason for joy
An

                         aNGEL

                         fROM

                          tHE

                         aSHES
```

Soulbait

You ran away before I could even say **goodbye**
If you think it's funny, look me in the eyes
Can't you   see from up there,
  how much of a **torture**d soul I've become?

          Forgive me
Bu t friend, I'm not done

It won't stop
Please...you know you were my **soul**mate
It won't stop

  Scream...I await th
e hook like hagfish **bait**

I cannot fill the grave with **agonic** monsters alone

Only your body will make this   hole a home
It's a
  sin
        that I can't take your place
I won't stop

                                          praying

God will a   ccept a trade

I stand looking down, as your **body lays**

I can't

believe

you stole my heart and my grave

I can't help but smell you in the fibers of my clothes

Fade away, please leave me alone, let go

Don't leave me alone

In this home, sweet hole

Your death, caught in my

throat

You know   , it's so cold

You left this

blue car in their *driveway*

But only **left** me   with

withered love notes

that I can never throw away

Kerosene

She's got candles in her
    throat
    Billowing out
            angels,
            ashes,
            and smoke
    Exhale with a
    million glances
            Light
            her
            up
with
                    heart-tipped   matches

Do you believe in me?

How do you put
love into words?
Is there any way to   describe the hurt?
To   chisel in the   coffin
                                          lid
All that you meant to
            him
  I'm doing the best I can
  Forgive me if I don't
          capture the

essence

The pain doesn't last forever, it's all temporary

Right now, you're looking through foggy glass

Objects in the mirror are more **precious** than they appear

today

I swear to you right now, look me in the eyes, it won't last

I'm taking my time to

spread

your

ashes

And set alight your   heart-tipped   matches

If there's a speck of air

Left in your   lungs

You know we   care

Fight for your life,

you're not done

Surrealist

till you've been hated	You can't love,
till you're degraded	You can't appreciate,
till you've cried	Can't smile,
till you've died	Can't live,

Answer me

Why do we sleep when we can't dream?

Tell me

That there's a light at the end, cause I can't see

what you've never fought	You can't survive,
till you've been taught	You can't know,

Comfort me

Give me something to cling to when the lights go out

Tell me

That when I go under you won't let me drown

Answer me

If I slip into the night would you hold my hand?

Tell me

That there will be a day I can stand

Promise me

That you won't **leave me** alone when I refuse to cry

Tell me

174

You're here for me until the day you die

Protect me

When I **feel them** closing in for the kill

Tell me

You will get me help before I make a wound that never heals

from myself...

Save me,

Iris

Hello, from Hell

Hope you're doing well

       Sunday can't kill me

       #5 fail

       Can you tell?

       I'm going pale

       Your funeral, beautiful

       Beyond this veil

Survivor's guilt is **bittersweet**

       Angels can't forgive

       <u>Shallow graves show **no** mercy</u>

Your bars will   set   me   free

                        Nothing

                        is

                        something

                        until I slit the rubber tubing

                        Terrible consequences to all the gears,

                        tears,

                        and fears using

                        Shows who knows who's gotta windpipe viewing

Spit my petals,

don't deny me

       Iris blink

like a

        beautiful

        disaster

                     in the works

I hear you really can't trust anyone

        after birth

        Eye lids

      Can't find me, shoulder length desert

     Think you know me?

     You have NO idea what I've seen

     You don't know **anything**

STOP,

     you don't know me

     So why do you think

     I owe you **anything**?

To reiterate my message

In conclusion, I repeat

     you don't know me

     So why would you have the audacity to think

     I owe you **anything**?

Sin-onym

This little cage
found deep inside
Cooping up everything
    that is bright
A sheet
draped over the crime
    Out of sight,
    and out of mind

      I can't ask you
      to forgive
Every one of
    my **SIN**s
Don't
think I'll try to
      defend
This past I   drag up
again and again
I'm tired of running
away
I'm tired of
refusing to say
Loneliness is
    a hard pill to take
But harder still are
      birthing pains

Should I leave and pray

                                    I don't lose

Every bit of me that's   inspired by   you?

Or should I stay

and risk knowing the truth?

There's nothing to say, and nothing to do

Flux

Hearts   beating

Never   sleeping

~~I'm kicked outta tomorrow~~

Fight the   flood

A plank of   wood

~~Will save us from the tide~~

Face a   need

Pump to   bleed

~~The sacred and the sorrow~~

I'm begging   you

Don't go   through

~~With your plan of anti-life~~

When faced against adversity

Flux is the only thing I can be

You **won't** get the better of me

Your hate don't mean ANYTHING

At your   feet

I'm begging,   please

~~I need to feel you inhale~~

It's killin'   me

To hear you   *scream*

~~I'm clinging to your agony~~

          Satisfy

Your   appetite

For the stains on the window

Don't   forget

Not worth the   spit

Won't sleep till you breathe

Curtain   time

I draw the   line

This is his final hour

Waited   long

To watch him   *crawl*

Away from where you lay

Fought for   you

Now see me   through

About to kill a coward

I'm not   done

Till he's strung   up

Satan better die today

If anyone happens to ask, I'm okay

There's absolutely nothing wrong, life is great

In fact, I'm **PEACHY**, hope you

noticed my smile

Perfect, inside and out, I'm a happy guy

Yeah, I'm thankful for everything I'm given

It couldn't be better, the life I'm livin'

Please believe I'm an   angel of a man

Please know that's exactly what I am

I promise, everything is   amazing

This isn't fake, this is u(n)changing

I could never be sad or upset

Cause life's so wonderful, it's so perfect

I don't wanna bring it up, I shouldn't say a thing

But if there was one complaint   that no one seems to see

I wouldn't call it a problem but I can't deny...

...I hate myself and wanna commit suicide

No   steps ta-ken backward
No   slowing up, slowing down
I will   never give in to you
IF   I push on, then you can't win
Why   do you surrender your life
For   someone else's agenda?
Fight for your Lord, love, and life
Push on,

PUSH

Eloi,

eloi,

lama sabactani

Survivor's Guilt, Pt. 1 (Dawn)

    ...And how have you survive   d
When you're only a lie
The whisper of a smile
First kisses, take time

    You are not alone, Alexandri   a
Survivor's guilt claims another, solace in pneuma
Bittersweet waves don't always play fair
I'll let you know when I get there

    Hold on tight to her, she is only here no   w
Life's good, until you're six feet underground
And if you love her, never let her go
If you truly love her, tell her so

    Find your heart in memories unknow   n
Wipe your tears, healing awaits beneath her stone
You knew her for only a moment of time
            But that moment
            will last
            your whole life

Survivor's Guilt Pt. 2 (Bittersweet)

It's such a cold dawn, dear, IT'S SO COLD

I wish I had ended with a

Hello

Survivor's guilt says GOODBYE is not a joke

It's bittersweet, the fade that won't go

       I pick my *fragile* way

through the stones

To find your name and to erase my own

Since   words

                   always

                    fail,

or so I am told

It's such a cold dawn, dear,

IT'S SO COLD...

Checkmate

I'm staring hard at the tears slithering down my face

Somehow I'm crying but I cannot feel anything

The Devil once again is calling my name

I'm too young to know that the pain eventually fades

Overdose, cutting, and asphyxiation

The attempts are piling up, chemical fornication

I've tried so many times and failed for only one reason

I'm loved others more than I love myself, how selfish does that make me?

I held on as long as I possibly can

Believe me, I've fought so hard against depression

And I know it's selfish of me to ask for a helping hand

So I'll keep it inside, till I run out of rope and be a man

I'm cold, in the shower, sobbing uncontrollably

Let's be real, this not how it's meant to be

I'll try again tomorrow and maybe eventually

I'll be found with a note in my fist stating "Checkmate" in sharpie

Pretty Monsters

Black stars and itty bitty bat wings

Suffocated, hydroplanin', twisted mini-things

Psychotic, apricot pit, suffrage

The voices tell me "I'm not

crazy yet"

Far from Sagittarius, *closer to*   *clowns*

DAD's deeds make this wo

        rld go round n' round

When I get to Heaven I'll tell

                JESUS

you said "Hi"

But if he says nothing,

            I won't ask why

Welcome to Hell

Hope you don't mind the smell...

No, we're not getting revenge

We just wanna be your friends

We don't want to

        fight

We're just here to drag you into the night

The morning mist,   microcosm

If you insist, I'll drag up the

past then

It's all my fault, there's   no denyin'

If you were velvet, I'd be **barbed wire**

The ugliest a   ngel I

  've ever seen

Has fallen right in front of me

We are the **lacerate**d   beauty ma rks

We are just...*pretty m0nsters*

Step into my **web**

You baby m0nsters

Step inside and I'll take good care of ya

Step inside of my ~~lies~~, promises hav   e been denie

d,

    fault de la

    vasfa

355

I hope you	're asleep
I hope you	can dream
I hope you	aren't thinking of me
I hope you	never forget how to breathe
	And
I hope you	...sing
If I can't	have sleep
	Maybe you can
If I can't	delete
	You stand a chance
If	there's any relief
	Cling to it tight
	So you never feel as alone as I feel
...tonight	

<u>Nudist</u>

I

--am the

---most selfish man

----that **ha**s ever lived...

ha ha ha

Sour risqué

This IS why I came

Draw me close   r

I c**ha**nged my

                        name

I'll never live

up

To your expecta-...

But I'll always c**ha**nge

day

        by

day

        by

day

        by

day

Take out your ridiCULe on me

Blame is my best friend

I'll be your scapegoat, som

eone **ha**s to

Acceptance is   shedding   skin

I like my life a little more **lifelike**

The

      twine

The

      swine

The

      line

T**ha**t swallows   all

the crown‑s sPine

Everyone t**ha**t said I'd fail was right

I'm great at

                                                    giving critique

But I just can't   take the heat

SuIcIde

And   tiny little lies

Fire up the   burner

I'm not getting any   younger

I never care until I'm underwater

I am a *nudist* in sheep's clo   thing

Scared the voices when I said "

                    You are crazy, and

there's nothing they can do to drag me down"

You weren't born with enough **pet**als to be worth my while

I sacrificed my

                                        time

-----Am I all you hoped I'd be?

Kiddie

Some will   argue,

some will   beg

Sweetie, not now,

                          daddy's making the bed

I need to beat in the cadaver's secrets

I wanna find   what's aching

I wanna find   something

                    That makes life worth living

                          I beat the hate in

So I can corrode what   she believes in

Kiddie in the pool, got a real good

            feel about it

                Salt the needles

                Stick my finger

                Swine are gearless

                Petals rub

                Drink my skin,

                eat my blood

I'm the little weasel who never knew when to give up

The Devil have no right to my   I refuse to surrender to
life   suicide

Give God a Gun

(I was born with ten fingers on the **trigger**)

Sugar skulls and lipstick in a tube
Scream FIRE in a crowded room

Shock   all the people
Stop   the disease when you're done
Shot   all the overkill
What   would happen if I

                  give God a **gun**?

The people that line the streets
 Looking everywhere just in case
      Sour skin, loose fingers
          The scent
        still lingers
Even though you're half a world away

No one's getting better
No one's getting worse

                Give God a **gun**
We all know the price is right
What's left to be done?
                Give God a **gun**
Lost it before we arrived

Cell block nine can't have all the fun

                        Give God a **gun**

If he pulls the **trigger,** would anyone blame him?

No one is that dumb

                        Give God a **gun**

There's an ache inside

You know it's right to   give God a **gun**

Superstit ion

No commiss ion

Narc otic

Patri otic

Nobody's gonna argue

with a planet sized **.45**

aimed at their head

Unlike you,   I
don't believe my heavenly father would pull the **trigger,** like
you did

to

him

Worm Diva

Pseudo-charismatic

Little boy with some lip-stick

Gonna   be a star some day

Gonna   make it somehow, some way

Violent   intentions

Masked   as   an   intervention

Gonna   learn respect one day

Gonna learn how to count his change

Cause   it's   gonna   unravel   before   it   unwinds
Yeah   it's   gonna   get   dark   before   it's   time
Crawl out of **your crevice** and
scrounge for a dime
If you wanna make a wish,
better make it count this time
No one's gonna accept you till you accept yourself
                              No,
there's no love out there if you can't get outta Hell
If you think you'll get lucky, you better find

                    somebody else
I'm
too scared of my-
_____ -self

Wash myself in all of
                                        your fear then
Make your *victims* my friends
When you told me
                        "Love
                is
            a
        lie"

I believed every word you said

Worm   diva
What do you do when no one's home?
Oh,   why
My   child
How will you survive in this world
all   alone?

                    I always hear "Nothing takes away the pain
                        Cause no one's here feels the same"

Introvert

```
                                    When I
force
away my
needs
                                    When I
refuse
all help for
me
Maybe someone else can s
                        e
                        e
Through the void of s
                      i
                      l
                      e
                      n
                      t e
                         y
                         e
                         s
Marking bodies, they pass by
I'll escape this prison b
                          l
                          i
                          n
                          d
```

Don't let me stay awake
　　too long
I remember
　　too much
to pass on

I was wrong to
disengage
I refuse to
believe
I embrace what's left   of me

Concentrate and dig your heels
Into the **dirt** that never yields
We never know what we feel
Falling faithfully,
　　　　　my call
Forever building up
　　　　　my wall
I erase the bath   room stall

Don't let me desecrate your   heart
With hollow threats and false   starts

　　　　　I
was wrong to turn the page
Simple

and u n c h a n g i n g

                        Foggy mirrors I am breaking

Don't let me in~~fil~~trate your mind

Too **ex**hausted to fade away into

t

h

e

night

R.T.A.

I await the collapse of today
Since we're here I thought I'd pray
There's something we can say
Before we begin to fade
Before we fade further away

I savor every hour
Be it sweet or be it sour
Somewhere soon, I will dissolve
Into a place that no plaster can form a wall

Don't let me violate your dreams
I will tear at the seams
Tear the seams, into the light
Don't let me desecrate your name
I was wrong to bring you pain
To bring you pain, in the dead of night

When I find something I'll never be
I have to respect the agony
When I single out the flaws that I see
I seem to respect the agony
After all these years, finally I feed
On what's left, respect the agony
I know now I cannot succeed
Without first choosing to respect the agony

Contradictions

I ~~got this killer idea a minute ago~~
~~Thought it's something you'd like to~~ know
~~So before~~ I ~~fell asleep I wrote it down~~
~~But when I~~ woke ~~up there were no words~~
The ~~paper was blank as the iceberg~~
~~Right before the~~ Titanic ~~pulled the trigger, without a sound~~

~~I'd like~~ to ~~think it was all a dream~~
~~That I imagined~~ this ~~whole thing~~
~~Maybe there was no~~ inspiration ~~after all~~
My ~~muse has been really shy~~
~~I don't have the~~ heart ~~to wake the guy~~
~~Yeah, I won't push him, I just sit and make sure he never~~ falls

~~I wanna sleep but~~ lately ~~I can't seem to get the knack~~
~~Or when~~ I ~~do sleep it's like an anti-insomniac~~
I fight ~~to meet my bed at a normal hour~~
~~But my bed lately doesn't seem~~ to ~~know I'm even there~~
~~So I fall to~~ sleep
And ~~sometimes I dream~~
~~They~~ write ~~letters to me~~
~~And~~ this ~~what I read~~

~~"There isn't~~ always ~~black and white~~
~~It doesn't~~ have ~~be hello or goodbye~~
~~Sometimes~~ things ~~aren't what they appear~~

~~There are lines~~ **that** ~~defy yes or no~~
~~Sometimes there's more than~~ **stop** ~~and go~~
~~But most people can't see this, I~~ **fear"**

Cuddling ~~with lights in the sky~~
~~Snuggling~~ **with** ~~stars and I~~
~~Never take anytime to ask~~ **her** ~~if I'm sane~~
~~I hate it when me~~ **and** ~~the moon fight~~
~~Cause neither~~ **her** ~~nor I will remember tomorrow night~~
~~The reason for the arguments, it's such a~~ **pain**

~~Might~~ **as** ~~well apologize~~
We ~~both know that you were right~~
~~I~~ **love** ~~the faces in the clouds~~
~~They stare back~~ **and** ~~they're so proud~~
~~I~~ **fall** ~~asleep~~
~~Sometimes~~ **I** ~~dream~~
~~I make~~ **believe**
~~Sometimes of~~ **you,** ~~I think~~

~~My alarm is set for two hours from now, so I close~~ **my** ~~eyes~~
~~And something tells me, the~~ **page** ~~won't be blank when I check next time~~

Haemolymph

Butte   **rflies** explode into b   lack souls as
            they float on the br   eeze

Violence   is a   beautiful
crime

Committed by aband   oned arsonis   ts

I would have you if   it was my choi   ce, but that paper
t   rail was stole n from me

Metamorp   **hosis,**
right in m   y livin   g room

Metamorphosis, like a dying flower   in full   bloom

You turn   ed to glass lik   e a bre
      athing figure

                                    ine
The carp   et, stai   ned red, a stain that
would never c   o

      me clean

Tack a st   ep back

O   ff the edg   e

Come with me..   .

Time r   aining across th   e
night sky

I am not a violent man, bu   t nei   ther
      r wa   s Charles Manson

            Towards this sullen br   anch in April, sick
      wi   th d   rippy sweat

204

It's no   w   here to
be foun   d,

                                        no

New Age Virgins

She's a   microcosm
She's a   cataclysm
She's my only way out and I aim to keep it that way
She's a   nihilist
She's a   synthesis
She's my escape from a grand existence, an innocent plaything

Cut her
Cut her   out of me
Just in case I ever wanted to learn how to breathe

Spiders crawl up
            out
              of
          the
        shower
            drain
Watching my every move   as   they   advance

Angels and devils
Bite and struggle
Forging ahead   like some sick S.O.B.'s
Pioneers of

                    The New Age Virgin Mary

So tuck it

Suck it in

Put on your best smile

And reach for

The Amer-I-can Dream

That flag seems a little out of reach

Maybe it's just me?

I'm no one in particular

I'm just   the forlorn

The appreciatively

torn

Perfect excuse to...

Wear me down

Wear my skin

Trophy of **sin**

Dead and lovin' it, follow through, and teach the incompetent
how to drown

New Age Virgins

Welcoming you to this mascara parade

New Age Virgins

Nowhere left to hide, lipstick macramé

New Age Virgins

Discriminate all the pretty abnormalities

New Age Virgins
Freedom is the only lie we need

So get up,

get out,

don't forget to pray to

your country,

your killers, and

your civil disobedience..
....
....
....
....
....
....
....
....
....
....
....
....
....
....
....The holy trinity of the...

Ape to Appetizer

Behind these closed e-y-e-s
Beneath this heavy crown,

    I hide

Rotten   and
stained but still

    alive

I eat my own kind to feed my   secret appetite

Rising like Satan's favorite

    appetizer

Rose colored apples

             and serpent legs scuttle, aimlessly

Souls   filled to the brim with mindless spiders

A corpse

in the back room, decaying like

        prostitution

      The Constitution

Becoming   kindling for the President's

        fireplace

And in the marketplace

Children starve and turn to breastfed

    devils

                                        Your defeat will come
                              slowly

Not swift like it could have

                                                        been
You chose the hard way out
Now there's absolutely no way out
          Underestimate the **ape**,
          and the angel will
          strangle what's left of the dead
And whatever you do, never forget

                                                  It's all
in your head
                                                  It's all
          that's left inside the abandoned cranium
Bombs built from orphans and widowed condemnation

Tell me   , when we didn't speak for days
That what I said   in my mind wasn't

                                                  a waste
                              You're never a waste

Chemical rain and P.T.S.D.
          The suicidal trees

Rainforest
appetizers

Just like   *me*

I AM   the Devil's

favorite midnight   snack

And **THAT**

                                                                    is

the

                                                              reason

I

                                                              attack

            My enemies are hollow angels

            Fallen from the throne room

            Swept aside with Adonai's broom

            My enemies are mason jars

            Waiting to be filled

Just waiting

Pep-talk

   Take a walk with me
Through the mire of choices
   Every day you make a choice
A choice to be brave
       To be strong
       To fight
       To not back down
Even with your face shoved in the ~~mud~~, you get back up

Shrug
it
off
And keep fighting
the
good
fight
Day after day
Year after year
You are truly
a   survivor
A   fighter
A truth writer
And you won't stop   **breathing**
Till your heart stops   **beating**

You...are...me...

And I am deeply proud of

you

Anxiety

Her love   is a snow swept December
Her love   is a never ending winter

It squeezes
It freezes

       Till I can't even breathe
       And I'm on the floor
       Begging for more
       I can't stop
       But I want to
As a fetus I rock
Back a n d forth
Trying   to stay (in)sane
Trying   to keep my brain
From abandoning me
I can't breathe

Her love   is a letter that ends it all
Her love   is a goodbye kiss just before the fall

It kills
It thrills

Until I can't even catch a break
And I'm

214

in

the

dirt

Begging to

hurt

To feel anything

      Anything

but this

This *angel* with frosted wings

Cold as her name, and the memories it brings

Caught out in the rain

                     A long, lonely walk to an empty home

                     Years of abuse have taken their toll

And I can't believe

        She

        would

        do

        this

...to me

Her love   is a fire that offers no heat

Her love   is a long night that surrenders no sleep

I can't breathe, because

Her love   reveals to me
Her name   is anxiety

Souvenirs

I wanna   DRAG
you away from this
But I can't force   YOU
to swim
All
I
can
do
is let go of your hand
And **pray** you kick as hard as you can

When these   WAVES
grow gray and start to pull you down
Pushing and pulling at your prayers,   DRIFTING
farther out
This
ocean
of
yesterday's,
makes you wanna give in
Just remember the days that you knew how to **breathe**

I know   LIFE
is covered right now in snow
But I promise it won't always be this   COLD
You won't always be fighting to keep your head above the surface

217

You

won't

always

fight

to sleep, fight to wake up, **fight** to get out and get dressed

Don't be so   AFRAID
to cry
We all need to shed   TEARS
if were gonna try
Live

in

the

moment,

remember there will always be nights like this

But I know there's a warm body out there waiting for someone
to share my crazy **life** with

Ghost

Synthesis of a spider's egg

No one worries if it's contained

But if we were to let them crawl in your pores

You'd never be the same

Matchsticks with little heads

Dolls made of human hair

Let's stick Molly inside the attic, then forget she was
there

Nobody blames the irritation on the innocent

Confide in a microphone, don't hate the consequences

Empty jaws break open well

Ever thought about writing a book about Hell?

Sciatic synthesis follows magazine sales

Cry it out and if you need to know, here's why I'm so pale

Closet encounters of the middle-class slaves

Too touchy of a subject so let's pray it goes away

Funny that you label the threads this way

Who's more obscene, hypocrites or the gays?

Here's some paper, write it down, what's on your mind?

The more you get it out, the less you have to hide

There's not a ghost alive that's dead inside

I see them all at night when I turn out the light

Everyone's a ghost, there's no surprise

Blinding auras of those who refused to die

I see them all when I close my eyes
The regret of your spirit is the last thing you'll see

Contraband

The suffocation of my literal mask

Tempting me away from everyone

Stagnate my fluidity

Cover my modest nudity

Tender, choice cuts of venison

Individual strands of my noose are made into *candle wicks* to keep the darkness legally blind

Blind, bloody, and sick of my *reject*ion

The cold nights are left to shiver by themselves

I refuse to feed your misery

If you really need someone, don't bother me

My monsters aren't under my bed

They fit just fine inside of my head

My skeletons need to accept their sexuality and come out of the closet

Sisters and brothers bathed in blood

Our favorite biography is now ***ill***egal contraband

Surrender your copies and sit down or join me and make a stand

The Powers That Be

Cannot stamp out us glowing coals

The Power That Means Everything

Has shaped us to burn under their soles

Grip

Take   your part in   the fi   e   lds

T   he gun   smo   ke of battl   e, tombs are   se   aled

Shad es of cri mson

Cat   ch   up w ith the livin'

Bea   ten d   own into gr   aves

S   o many hav   e fal   l   en, few remain

     Nigh ts   spent trying to   repai   r, all in vane

So man   y   hav   e   fallen   a   way

     Hold   on   to eac   h oth er

We do   n't have muc   h time t   ogeth   er

Be t   han   k   ful, my   bro   ther s

Do not dou   bt, or   be consumed by t   he river

Unspoken

I'm peering through a shattered window
My life hits its grand crescendo
Nothing left to do but say goodbye
My last request, just a fleeting wish
Is no one ever feel like this
I can't forget the fire in your eyes
Cause something is dead inside
It never feels like I'm alive
If I'm talking crazy, take me away
But I'll keep screaming your name
Till someone turns out the lights

Little hopes, they're paper thin
Drag me back home again
Suicidal prayers seem lost in the sky
Fluent in this bitter language
If I'm not clear, send me a message
With one last breath I'll know we survived
Day by day, hour by hour
Don't forget your father's flowers
I need to watch them bloom again
I need to smell their decadence
I need this message to be received
I need to remember how to breathe
Oh, you lift me up
And oh, then you let me fall

I stayed down as long as I could

    I pushed and pulled at heartstrings till I spent me last cent

Burnt up my last drop

    Sucked in my last hit

Left you all behind just so I could learn how to love myself

I couldn't care less if I survived

    I just watched it all fade away

Limbs growing so numb

    No note, no hint, a lifetime of things to say

    Where regretful thoughts go to die

    That's where you'll find

    What's left of my life

        Some storms weren't made to drag away everything you had

        How many times have I given in to the cold front at hand?

    Please don't tell me I'll be fine

    If I wanted to hear that I'd ask for another lie

    One more goodbye

That's all I ask, please fade my bruise

    Silence as they auctioned off my mind

All I ask, please, fill in the blank "I love _____."

Indelible

Here in the ink I lay

And again I hear his whisper in my ear

Those words

Those words

Those words vomiting agony and selling it as wine or holy water

A promised cure for cancer that is only a pretty, red placebo

But right now I'll believe anything, buy anything, take anything, do anything...to ease the pressure, the ache, the burn, the bruising...the snag beneath my skin

Here in the ink I lay

Sucking in the sticky stench of an unwashed body (maybe a week, maybe longer)

Un-brushed teeth (the surfaces smothered in swampy plaque)

The same clothes I've had on for 5 days straight, my pillow, sheets, and blankets becoming a second skin as I surrender to hopelessness in my personal cesspool of cotton and polyester

Here in the ink I lay

His whispered words, so gentle and kind

Such a trustworthy liar

Such a generous thief

Such an affectionate serial killer

His voice is honey

But his words are cyanide

Maybe I don't have a purpose

Maybe there is no relief

Maybe the beliefs I've held onto for dear life, for so long, are simply a fallacy of faux smiley faces and summer breaks long since buried in the loam...worm food...dead

No coffin

No headstone

No funeral procession

None of those memories felt as real as the cylindrical, pumpkin orange bottle filled to the tippy top with tiny, tiny yellow, football shaped pills

Xanax

Each one of them .5 milligrams of muscle relaxant medication

Easy to get, easy to swallow, easy to overdose on if you know your body's limitations

You just double that number and you know approximately how much it takes to slow your heartbeat to a lethal BPM

In 15-20 minutes you will be unconscious and shortly after, your heart will pack up, shut off the lights, and go out of business

Here in the ink I lay

These words floating in my mind's stratosphere

Yet something stirs inside and I remember that somehow it's Wednesday again

And against all odds I grudgingly slide out of bed, make my way out the door, into my car, and end up on the West Side, the sun, a bloodshot eye, it's lid began to close over Evansville, Beyond the Veil pulsating in my peripheral vision

Sitting in the parking lot, I find no desire or point in going inside, but the stirring is too strong, and I'm beyond fighting

Like livestock to the barn, not knowing why, not caring, just seeking warmth, I clip clop inside

Here in the church I sit

Sponging the active atmosphere, half-listening to the chirping of bible birds

I don't want to be here

I don't need to be here

I'll leave soon

The discussion on gifts of the spirit tastes bitter to me

Too bitter

Maybe I'm tasting myself?

This doesn't matter to me

I don't want to be here

I don't need to be here

I'll leave soon

The deeper the discussion, the deeper the bitter distaste

Oh, I agree with the conversation and it's many accurate comments that slithers around the room

It does nothing for me though

It doesn't wake me up inside

It doesn't help me feel alive

I'm still going to do what I gotta do later tonight

And NO ONE, and NOTHING is gonna stop me

The stirring flutters again

I don't want to be here

I don't need to be here

I'll leave NOW

As my calf muscles tense to raise me out of the couch's cushion company that I confuse with comfort...I'm pushing myself up to walk out, when a woman says something from God that shot straight down my spine, another woman says my name and gives me another message from God, and another, and another

They ask if they can pray for me

Can I say no?

Dare I say no?

The men and women's hands pummel me like an avalanche of prayer, some plead for shields deep inside, some speak aloud and alive

The depression (they pray), will not take my life tonight

The anxiety (they pray), will not chain me down

The pain (they pray), will strengthen me rather than destroying my faith

They call out The Enemy on everything he is doing to me

Something in my chest is exhaled...something thicker than oxygen

I tremble

They call out The Enemy on his plans to take my life, for he knows that he must attack the largest threats with the strongest demons

Something in my chest burns as it is forced from my lungs...thick, clotting fumes

I gag and shake

Tears I've fought back for so long well up and spill onto the carpet

The bitter hate evaporates as my lungs (never more than half full) suck in breath after breath of The Holy Spirit

Crashing waves

Surging maelstrom of love

I whisper "Daddy, daddy, daddy..." over and over as I am consumed in his embrace

My eyes, now opened both physically and spiritually drank in the vibrancy of the light and brilliance of color and sound

After the Amen's were whispered, in the silence that follows, electricity flows through my veins, peaks and valleys of goosebumps in my skin

Overwhelmed, hearing the words of encouragement, I let my auto-pilot take over and thanked everyone that approached me

Hugs

Love

Stay strong bub

I leave shortly thereafter

Hardly saying a word to anyone, although they said so much to me

And now, as I write this

Here in the ink I lay

Freshly showered, teeth brushed, new clothes, new sheets, and...new heart

I feel so clean, lily white

Inside and out

Purged and unoppressed, lungs full of the same air that breathed life into dust so long ago

Because I crawled out from my comfortable discomfort

And because a dozen women and men did as God led them, I lay in this ink, and toss the pill bottle in the trashcan next to my bed

I'm turning off my light, and going to sleep, knowing that I will wake up in the morning and I will use my new pen and blank page of paper

And I will put a bullet hole in that voice that whispers in my ear with every word I write

Satan...

You should've killed me when you had the chance...

The beginning.

Thank you, my dear readers, for joining me tonight, and for staying until the curtains were drawn. I pray that you soaked in some redeeming messages, both consciously and subconsciously that will aid you on your way home through the voids between street lamps. From the bottom of my soul I thank you. Good luck, go safe, and God bless.

Dydda is a young spirit who has dedicated his life to crafting hope and beauty from within the dark depths of depression, anxiety, and Bipolar Disorder that afflicts him. He is a writer, poet, musician, and beloved son of his heavenly father. His only wish is for others to be saved from suffering, if only for a moment. This is his second collection of poetry.

Made in the USA
San Bernardino, CA
10 July 2018